MW01175132

A Woman Sold and Other Poems

A WOMAN SOLD

AND

OTHER POEMS.

A WOMAN SOLD

AND

OTHER POEMS.

BY

AUGUSTA WEBSTER.

London and Cambridge:
MACMILLAN AND CO.
1867.

CAMBRIDGE:
PRINTED BY C. J. CLAY, M.A.
AT THE UNIVERSITY PRESS.

CONTENTS.

	PAGE
A WOMAN SOLD:—	
I. ELEANOR VAUGHAN	1
II. LADY BOYCOTT	14
ANNO DOMINI 33:—	
I. BARTIMÆUS	38
II. JUDAS	42
III. PILATE	53
IV. THE WALK TO EMMAUS	68
THE OLD YEAR OUT AND THE NEW YEAR IN	74
IN THE STORM	78
NEVER AGAIN	80
GOING	81
THE RED STAR ON THE HILL	82
A MESSENGER	85
THE RIVER	87
TWO MAIDENS	89
THE GIFT	90
IF?	91

PAGE

THE HEIRESS'S WOOER 94

DEAD AMY 96

A MARCH NIGHT 98

THE HIDDEN WOUND 99

SAFE 101

PASSING AWAY 102

TOO FAITHFUL 104

SHADOW 107

SUNLIGHT 108

A MOTHER'S CRY 109

DREAMING 112

A WEDDING 113

THE SETTING STAR 114

TO ONE OF MANY 115

LOOKING DOWNWARDS 117

ON THE LAKE 119

TO AND FRO 120

AFTERWARDS 123

OUR LILY 125

ON THE SHORE 127

GLAD WAVES 128

DESERTED 129

PERJURED 132

HOW THE BROOK SINGS 134

THE LAKE 135

PAGE

In the Sunshine 138

Night Whispers 139

The Blush-Rose 142

A Bride 143

Mary Lost 144

The Land of Happy Dreams 145

The Shadow of a Cloud 146

Fairies' Chatter 147

Lota 199

ERRATUM.

Page 81, line 5. *For* the stillness *read* a stillness.

A Woman Sold.

I.

ELEANOR VAUGHAN.

Lionel. Then it is true!
Eleanor.   Oh Lionel, you look
So strangely at me. Think, I all alone,
So many reasons, all my friends so fain,
My mother pressing me, Sir Joyce so good,
So full of promises, he who could choose
No bride among the highest ladies round
But she would smile elate and all her kin
Bow low and thank him and go swelled with pride —
You cannot wonder that my friends declare
They'll hear no Noes, but force me to my good.
Lionel. No, 'tis at you I wonder. Eleanor,
When first I heard this lie—I called it so
In anger for you, I will call it so,
Though your lips contradict me, till the last

Worst proof have sworn it other, 'tis so strange,
So recklessly untrue to that pure self
Of my love Eleanor—When first I heard
That lie on you, as if you, a young thing
In the bud of stainless girlhood, you the like
Of babies in your fond grave innocence,
You proud as maidens are who do not know
What sin and weariness is like in lives
Smirched by the pitch that seethes, they've told you, far
From your balm-scenting nostrils, but perceive
Yourselves are as the high accessless snows
Whose blushings do but prove their perfect white,
And so look coldly down on something base,
You know not what, beneath you—you whose smiles
Are gladder than most laughters, and whose voice
Rings like the wild birds' singing in the wood,
Because you are so young and new in heart,
You who to me—

        But say, to put the least,
You, the Miss Vaughan we men agree to think
Worth anyhow such common reverence
As good girls like our sisters have from us—
That you were bought like any lower thing
Our Crœsus fancies, like the horse that won
The Derby last, the picture of the year,
The best bred pointer, or the costliest ring;
You bought by such a buyer, a cold fool
Whose very vices, like his polished airs,

His tastes and small-talk, were acquired by dint
Of callous perseverance; one who'll own,
With a feigned yawn, he's something bored with life,
Meaning by life stale sins and selfishness;
A dried up pithless soul, who, having lacked
The grace to have a youngness in his youth,
Now lacks the courage to be old—You bought
For laces, diamonds, a conspicuous seat
In country ball-rooms, footmen, carriages,
A house in town and so on—and no doubt
Most liberal settlements, that is but just.
A man past youth and practised out of tune
For loving should not haggle at the price
When he buys girlhood, blushes, sentiment,
Grace, innocence, aye even piety
And taste in decking churches, such fawn eyes
As yours are, Eleanor, and such a bloom
Of an unfingered peach just newly ripe.
Aye, when a modest woman sells herself
Like an immodest one, she should not find
A niggard at the cheque book.
                        Eleanor,
Can I not *taunt* you even to a no?
Look up ; defend yourself. Oh ! you sit there
Languid and still, and grow a little pale,
And flush a little, and will not reply
Even by a look. Be angry with me, child,
Cry out that I misjudge you to my shame ;

Say I, like a rough lawyer, questioned you
Into a maze, and twisted me a yes
Out of your shifting coil of noes, while you
Were dimly pondering what I asked. Speak, speak;
Say anything, but do not let me break
My passion on you while you droop and give
Like a rock-rooted seaweed in the surf.
Say anything, except that I do well
To speak to you as I have spoken now.

Eleanor. Ah well! you do no ill that I can chide.
I, who have gladly let you give me praise
Far past my merit in the foolish time
When I believed I could grow like your praise,
Must bear in patience now if you give blame
Perhaps a little harder than you know.

Lionel. So humble, Eleanor! How you are
        changed—
What is it? Are you ill? You were so proud.

Eleanor. Yes, that was long ago before I knew
I could be *tempted* even to do wrong.
You know my boast was that I never broke
The lightest merry promise. Long ago
I could be proud.

Lionel.   Be proud again, my love,
My Eleanor! I know you are yourself
When you speak so. Be proud again, too proud
Not to atone. Stay, shall I tell you, dear,
How I received the tidings that Miss Vaughan

Was pricked for Lady Boycott? Why, I laughed,
Laughed, Eleanor, as any schoolboy might
Who heard his awful doctor had been caught
Picking a small boy's pocket for his pence.
It was not long ago. Young Polwarth came
To town, dined with me at our club, and there
Tossed out his precious news quite innocent
Of where it touched. "Miss Vaughan!" I laughed,
       "The joke
Is too far-fetched. You do not know her well."
Till he, abashed, recanted, "Well, no doubt
The rumour is not true; but so it runs."
And later that same evening Pringle came,
And he—I think he knew he stung me—yes
He'd guessed why his sweet speeches forced a clash
Of discord in your ears, where other words
Were making your love music—he was loud
With the same story. "Aye," he said, "she's wise,
That coy Miss Eleanor, she knows her worth.
All very well to lure on you or me
With her odd ways, half peacock and half dove,
Strutting and cooing—but, for marriage, why
We come to business then. She's a shrewd girl."
And *he* would not recant: he'd swear 'twas true.
But I said, "You'd not play fool's trumpeter
To the idiot gossips who invent such trash:
No surely: You and I both know her well."
And, Eleanor, even now I say to you,

It is not true—I know it who know you.

    Eleanor. Yes long ago you knew me, but not now.

    Lionel. And when was long ago? A second time
You talk of long ago. Not three months past
Since we last parted, and I took your word
Of sorrow-sweet good bye away with me
To be my sweetest memory, and thought,
"I shall succeed because she loves me so,"
And turned me to my crabbed toil, as if
It had been some romance of a true love
That thrills the reader through—some rare romance
With your name in it, Eleanor, and mine,
And a glad end. You call this long ago,
And I still live in it, live in the life
Your love—the dream of your love was it?—gave.
What long ago? Not all a year by days
Has passed since first a sudden moment broke
My silence—ours. You looked me a reproach,
Not knowing how you looked, how pleadingly,
For a light word I spoke—as a man speaks
Who plays with his own heart and pricks at it
To prove because he laughs it does not feel—
A jest as if I thought gay scorn of love
And prized a woman as we prize a rose,
Meaning all roses and the one in hand,
All liked with just a difference for taste
In perfumes and in tints. You looked at me:
And I at you. How could I help it, child?

I had remembered on for weeks and months
That I was a poor man and should not speak,
But I forgot it just a moment long,
Because you had forgotten, and my eyes,
Hungry for one love look, met yours so full
That you grew red and trembled, and I knew
In a quick impulse that you were my own,
And that I had no life which was not you.
And I said, breathless—what, I do not know,
But something that meant "love me," and you raised
Your quivering face with a strange radiance on it
Of tenderness and promise and grave joy,
And looked into my eyes, and said no word,
But laid your hand in mine. And then you wept
Because—'twas you that said it, Eleanor—
Because you were so happy. And I drew
Your head against my breast, and whispered "wife,"
And you—oh sweet and simply loving girl
And natural—you put your lips to mine
And kissed me. Oh! my wife that was to be,
My Eleanor, was that day long ago,
That day which always is my yesterday?

Eleanor. No, no, you must not talk to me of that,
You must not. There are things one must forget—
One should at least. But ah! it is so hard.
One must be happier than I can be
To be able to forget past happiness.
But, Lionel, what you call yesterday

Seems to me parted from my present self
By a whole other life lived in the dark,
I know not when. Ah! surely yesterday
Is long ago when all its hopes are dead,
And Eleanor is dead who lived in it
And loved you—oh *did* love you. Do not think
I am all heartless. I *did* love you more
Than you will know now ever.

        Let me go,
Let go my hand—not now—oh! Lionel,
We are not each other's now.

 Lionel.   *Did* love me, *did?*
Is *that* a long ago too? My own love
You love me now. Yes love me. Look at me.
You'll keep your faith. You dare not say again
We are not each other's now.

 Eleanor.   You hold my hand;
Look what you hold with it—it hurts me now
In your tight grasp, and it has hurt ere now
With another kind of pain. But bye and bye
I shall grow used to it. It means, you know,
My fetter to the hus—— to him, Sir Joyce,
Who will be soon—I suppose I am his now,
Marked by his ring.

 Lionel.   There, take your hand again.
It *is* his for the moment. It was mine
By a less unholy bargain. Answer me,
Do you love your happy lover, Eleanor Vaughan?

Eleanor. He is kind. A good wife always gives her love
To a kind husband.

Lionel.   Aye, some women can;
Not you.

Eleanor. Sir, though I have done wrong to you,
And so have humbled me before your scoffs,
I am a woman, as I think, not like
To fall short of my duty as a wife.
Be sure Sir Joyce will have his due from me.

Lionel. Yes, crane your neck in the old way,
        flash down
Superb bright scorning from your hooded eyes.
Wife's duty, yes, you'll never shame that, child;
You'll make this sin of yours shine out at last
Like virtue by your married perfectness.
I can believe it. But you'd make me laugh,
Were't not for shuddering that you are so fooled
To your blind venture by a moral shred
Of heartlessness. "Kind husbands make good wives,
And good wives love their husbands"—very sage—
And prudent mothers preach it to their girls,
And the pith of it is "Do not choose by love,
But look to means; because a man who's poor
Must be unkind, for want of cash to spend
Upon his wife." And so you're all agreed,
You and your family, Sir Joyce will be
A model husband, (he's so rich), and make,
By paying bills, and giving jewelry,

The typed good wife of you. But do you think,
You who at least have known that loving means
A something more than Thank yous, than replies
Of a civil sort, and easy going smiles,
And a fattening placid womanly goodwill
To a comfortable master, can learn now
To cheat your heart with such a dull content,
And be at rest and bask? You, Eleanor!
You'll pine to love as a caged sparrow pines
To fly, you'll tear and break your useless wings
With beating at the bars, or else you'll mope
In obstinate tired stillness; you'll not thrive
On caged birds' food, and sing. Oh! you are mad.
You do not know yourself. Oh! child, be warned.
Why will you curse your youth with such a life?
Nay, let me speak to you—let me speak still.
I have not spoken to you of myself:
I would not beg for mercy, let you find
What a poor quivering wretch a man may be
Before the little blow from a light hand
That breaks his heart: I dared not even say
"Tis something hard on me," lest I should bare
A foolish throbbing anguish for myself
'Twere fitter to keep hidden, and should shock
Your cold ear with such outcry for the pain
As shames a man. But I will tell you once
Because, since you still love me, I believe
It may a little move you, I endure

More grief in this than—

                     Child, I cannot do it!
I cannot. Oh! the passion will have vent.
Aye, if one could dissect one's living heart
And lecture coldly on it, I might speak
In sober phrases and set out my grief
With due pathetic touches, till perhaps
You'd weep a little for it. Now 'tis I
Who shed a fool's weak tears. Yes, keep your head
Turned from me; you are wise, for if you looked
You might remember, were't but in a mood
Of foolish pity, that I am the man
Who trusted you, set all his hopes on you,
Because he had your promise, loved you past
All thought of treachery from you. Aye, there,
There in one breath is the whole agony,
I love you.

    Eleanor. Oh my love! Oh, my own love!
Forgive me, help me.

    Lionel.   Yes, press your dear arms
Still round my neck, close, so. My Eleanor,
You are my own again, is it not so?

    Eleanor. Yes, yes.—I cannot tell—Oh Lionel,
Do help me. Tell me what to do.

    Lionel.   My love,
My promised wife, we stand together now;
They shall not part us with their formal rules.
I gave my word, till I could come to them,

"I am rich enough to ask your leave again,"
I would not take aloud the right you gave
And say "she is for me," nor ask to break
The weariness of absence with one word
Written to bid you think I worked for you,
Nor one dear answer that you loved me still.
"No letters, no engagement." I bore all,
And kept my faith. They've kept no faith with me:
And now I face them. Love, can you be firm
And wait? Wait, not for such a wealth and rank
As shall be Lady Boycott's at the Hall,
But for a simple home where things are smoothed
By love more than by spending, for a life
Where little cares go plodding hand in hand
With little pleasures?

    Eleanor.   Lionel, I know
I could be happier so—with *you*—I know,
Than in the tempting paradise Sir Joyce
Has won my parents with—and almost me.
Ah! love, I have been weak. You were away.
And I was flattered. And I had gone far
Before I knew where I was being led.
It seemed too late at last. But I am yours:
I have come back to you. Yes I will wait
For always.

    Lionel.   Dear, it need not be for long,
If you will take a poor man, but half way
To where he hopes to reach. I'm prospering, love.

I shall not win for long what was to be
My goal for claiming you, the promised prize ;
But I take answer now from none but you,
And, very soon I hope, I shall return .
And say "Come now, for there is room for you
In a fit home which I have earned." But, love,
You will be strong?

   Eleanor.   Yes ; but you must not go,
You must be near me.

   Lionel.   Nay, dear, I must work.
Clients and causes stand no truanting :
And I am greedy now to heap up gains.
Oh ! darling, I am sad to leave you here
In your changed churlish home. You will not find
Much kindness in it now?

   Eleanor.   *You* will be kind.

   Lionel.   Oh, darling ! oh, my love won back to me !
Cling to me once again. My Eleanor !
Sir Joyce can never buy my wife away.

   Eleanor.   Oh never, never. Love, I *will* be strong.

A Woman Sold.

II.

LADY BOYCOTT.

Lady Boycott. Yes, dear; come in. I was but
     looking out
At the soft twilight slowly growing specked
With those white stars. A dreamy sort of time
This is, and one forgets the clock goes on
While one is watching stillness so. I fear
I seem discourteous keeping thus apart;
I did not mean it.
    Mary.   And I did not think it.
Only your journey has been long—I feared
You might be over weary.
    Lady B.   I am tired.
I am always tired, I think. Shall we be missed
Beyond forgiveness if we sit awhile
Here in this quiet, you and I alone,

And dream a little as we used to do
In the old idle days when we were young?

 Mary. *Were* young! Why I feel nearer to a child
And feel life newer now than when I went,
With all our school-girl ladylike grave airs
And necessary stateliness still worn
With the gloss not yet rubbed off, to play my part
Of bridesmaid to my classmate Eleanor—
Some months I think my elder. Then it seemed
As if months told in age. Do they count still?
That was six years ago, and I am young:
And are you old?

 Lady B. Ah! well, you laugh at me.
But I count years by length of heavy days.
It is so different—a girl's time goes
Like music played for dancing; but a wife's—
Ah Mary married women soon grow old.

 Mary. Love is itself a youth; they should be young
Until their husbands die.

 Lady B. And mine is dead.

 Mary. Dear Eleanor! My foolish sudden tongue!
What was I thinking of?

 Lady B. Why not of me.
You had forgotten me, I saw, just then.
Mary, you need not play now at belief
That the happiness of wifely love was mine—
Such love as we believed in when we talked
In our dear wont here, oh! so long ago,

In such soft dusk as this, of what should be
And what should not to make up that pure good
Of loving and of being loved again.
Mary, you know I never loved Sir Joyce.
   Mary. Oh Eleanor! I feared it. But indeed
I think you should not say it—even now.
    Lady B. Oh let me say it, friend, sweet secret
      friend,
Who will not babble it to the four winds
To have them blow it through the neighbours' homes.
Let me speak but to you, I who have smiled
A cheating silence for so many years.
You do not know the penance to be good
And pretty mannered dull day by dull day,
Lapping one's heart in comfortable sloth
Lest it should fever for its work, its food,
Of free bold loving. No, you cannot dream
How one may suffer just by doing right
When in one's heart one knows how under right,
For base of it, there lies a stifled wrong
Which is not dead. Ah me! wrong never dies.
You lay it underground, you tread your path
Smoothly above it, then you build new hopes,
New duties, new delights, upon its grave—
It stirs and breaks up all. And, worse than this,
Mary, you cannot kill old happiness—
No not except by heaping new upon it—
And you remember in your heavy heart

The sweetness of delicious unwise days
Left with your young girl follies—with your doll,
Your poetry, your dreamings, and your love;
Irrational light pastimes.
   Mary.   Hush, oh! hush.
I never like you in your flouting moods.
You shall not scorn yourself so. Weep, dear, weep,
If you are sad, and bid me comfort you,
But let be with that jarring heartlessness.
'Tis bitter acting, dear, when grief puts on
A show of laughters and makes mirth by scoffs.
   Lady B. Aye, you were right to hush me. Let
      me have
The ease of free complaining. There's no fault
If I look dull-eyed now, no secret told.
'Tis only loveless wives who must not fret,
For fear of being understood—indeed
For fear of understanding their own selves.
But I, alas! there has a new thing chanced,
And forced myself upon me. I have burst
My serious due disguise of widowhood.
I am bold now with my sorrow. Why indeed
Should I talk shadows to myself or you
Who know the shape of truth behind them? Yes,
You read my secret, Mary, years ago:
You, with your show of taking me at what
I should have been, an easy-minded wife
Who loved her lord in quiet and was pleased

2

To have her comforts with him...or without;
You, with your silent tenderness, your talk
Of making duty dear by loving it
For God's sake, if not man's—you knew the while,
I saw it, you kind prudent hypocrite,
That I was wearier than the worn drudge
Who toils past woman's strength the hard day through
And cowers at evening to the drunken boor
Who strikes her with a curse because she's his
And that's his right upon her—wearier
Because my labour was to love against
The longings and the loathings of my heart,
Because the price I earned was only smiles
And too familiar fondlings. Ah! he had
His rights upon me. And he meant me well.
He was not often hard to me; he gave
With an unstinting hand for all my whims,
And tricked me with the costliest fineries
Almost beyond my wish; was proud of me
And liked to look at me, and vaunted me,
My beauty and my grace and stateliness,
My taste and fashion. What could he do more?
We were not suited; some more fitting wife—
Say one who could have loved him, for that makes
The only fitness—one whom years or care
Had brought a little nearer to his age,
Enough to crave no more than was in him
Of sympathies and high ideal hopes;

One who had never loved, or could forget
How the young love, and could bestow on him
A fond contented kindness for the sake
Of his meant kindness to her; such a wife
Might have enjoyed in him a better calm
Of meet companionship than I could find,
Might have shared with him little daily thoughts
And answered when he talked and not felt dull,
Nor missed-- you do not know him I *did* love;
You do not know all that there was to miss.
I cannot make you feel that for me. Well,
As for Sir Joyce, doubtless if he had used
A cruel tongue against me, cruel smiles
And frowns, or cruel hands, I must have been
Only more wretched; though I'd wildly think
Often and often I could draw free breath
Rather beneath a bad harsh tyranny,
Coming from him, than kindness and his smile
And condescending husbandly caress.
He made me feel so abject and so false
When he approved me so! Why, I have longed
To shriek "No, hate me, I am false to you,"
And have him think me fouler than my fault.
And yet I dreamed, not loving him, I loved
No other then. I thought my heart at least
Had numbed to an unsinning deadness. Yes,
I did in truth believe I had full learned
The difficult strange lesson to forget,

Because I would not, could not think of *him.*
Because I had no lover, I believed
I had no love.

    Mary.   Oh ! my poor Eleanor,
I stop you once again. You run too wild
In your regrets. I know you had no love,
Except as one may love the dead. You were
A weary woman plodding on alone,
Thinking sometimes " Alas I might have gone
A fairer way and held a guiding hand
Warm within mine," and sometimes looking back
Too sadly on the old bright time of love,
As in your age you might look back on youth ;
But you had no fond passion quick in you
To make a fever in your heart. That pulsed
Too slow and chilly. You were faint because
You had foregone the love on which it lived,
And you knew that. But, dear, you let the love
Go with the lover, mourning for them both.
I could read that much, plainly.

    Lady B.   Well, may be
You read it rightly, and I did not dash
My forced cold wifely duty with that blot.
I'll hope it. But there has a new life come
And joined on to the old that was before
My bargain with Sir Joyce, and now it seems
As if there had been scarce a break between—
Only a troubled rest, as when one tries

To wake and cannot, and yet does not sleep.
I cannot count you "Look, so many days,
Or years, or moments even, I was pure
From present loving." I feel only this :
There is a man I know whose whisper was
To me all promise of the future days,
All sweetness of the present; and there is
A man who with one cold and civil look
Has broken me, has made me sick of hope
Because he is not in it, made my life
Too flickering to be worth the care it costs;
And they are one, and they are my one love.
Oh! Mary, darling, comfort, comfort me.
Yes, hold me to you, let my head lie so.
Yes, soothe me, love me, darling—Oh my friend
I need another love than yours, *his* love.
I want it, want it.
   Mary.   Dear, dear Eleanor.
Ah! you are hurt past help of mine. I would
I had this lover here : he should not keep
A placid conscience. But, dear, be too proud
To let him break you. If he, years ago,
Must win a girl's weak heart to toss it back,
A plaything you might hand on to Sir Joyce
While he should choose some other—
   Lady B.   Mary, No.
I was the one who wronged our truth—I, I.
He was all truth.

Mary.   Ah! now I understand
That you are sad beyond the help of tears.
Poor heart, how shall I soothe you.   Ah! you tore
The blossom of its hope with your own hand,
And then you hunger in a barren day
Because it bears no fruit.   Dear sorrower,
What can I say?   Take courage.   Not a life
So lonely in this world but somewhere grows
A blessing for it out of other lives,
And warmth out of their fire-light.   Not a soul
So lonely under heaven but it may reach
The hand of God, and lift itself from pain.
Take courage, dear.

    Lady B.   No, let me break my heart.
Would he had never loved me—only that,
Not to remember that he loved me once.

    Mary.   But, Eleanor, he may remember too.
Truly you did him such a bitter harm
As well may make a man grow hard and strong
Against a woman's sobbings, battling back
The vain breath of her words like a barred tower
Careless to the wild useless gusts of winds,
Silent against them.   Yet, for the dear sake
Of what you were to him and he to you,
And for the likeness of your face to that
He loved to look on once, which smiled on him
With so unlike a smile, and for the thought
That you might be yourself again through him,

And for the sorrow constant in your eyes,
He might put by his rancour, might tune down
The bitter tongue of blame to just a strain
Of pity for himself who had lost you,
Until 'twas pity for you too, and so
He must forgive you.

  Lady B.   Oh! your idle hopes!
It is as if you'd mock me. They were mine.
I shaped them for myself—such pretty dreams!
Like what one sees in clouds—and then the wind,
The lightest breeze that scarce can stir a leaf,
Will float them into nothings. Why, you give
My folly a clear voice, and make me laugh
To think how crookedly its answer falls
To the plain question of my wretchedness.
He *does* forgive me, has no rancour left,
Has quite forgotten bitterness and blame,
Doubtless would pity me if he but cared
To know if I am sorry or content—
He'd pity me out of his chivalry,
Because I am a woman. But he looks
Unmoved upon me, doubtless would allow
" Her face is fair, she has an easy grace,
Was most attractive, though now something worn;"
And there's an end of it. I am to him
At most the faded picture of a girl
Whom he once wished for but could teach himself
To do without, and so for that, because

All memory which is not pain is sweet,
And for the courtesy of gentlemen
To well-bred women, he'll sit by my side
And chat a little, give a gracious laugh
At my tart sayings, talk of the last news,
Ask some one sitting near if he agrees
With Lady Boycott's judgment on the point,
And go to be as civil to the next
Upon his list of doll acquaintances.
Forgive me! Blame me! Why, he'll meet my eye
With a friend's carelessness, will smile at me
The perfect proper smile of drawing-rooms.
Oh! my lost love! one love of all my life!
He cares no more for me than for the weed
In flower against his foot, that, if he has time,
He'll notice "In its way 'tis well," and pass,
Just stepping so as not to trample it,
Because he's kindly natured and would crush
No poor slight growing thing without a need.
He cares for me no more than for the dream
He dreamed in last night's sleep, and waking lost:
No more than for the queen in pinafores
Loved in his days of slate and spelling-book.
I am nothing to him, nothing—oh, my love!
And I to shiver in the cold he makes
And smile to him! Mary, I sometimes wish—
Yes, wish, as some sick wretch will idly moan,
"Give me sharp pangs rather than this dull pain,"—

I might go mad a moment, lose the sense
Of womanhood, and let his cold man's eyes
See to my heart, see my unhonoured love.
Not that he'd love me then—no never that—
But that there'd be some bond between us then,
Or some defiance, not this civil show,
This mannerly kind hateful indifference.
At least he'd be ashamed for my shame, drop
His eyes that look on me so cold and pleased
At our next meeting, stammer when he spoke.
Perhaps he'd shun me. Aye, and at the least
I could shun him. Now I dare never wince,
Nor stand a step back from a meeting, lest
He should discover.

   Mary.   But, my Eleanor,
Since all he knows is that you long ago
Took back your love, were it not possible
That he should silently be measuring
The present with the past and noting down
The unconscious signals?

   Lady B.   Not another word,
Not one smooth word of hope. When he did love
I knew before he spoke—half knew, I think,
Before he knew it. Now I as well know
He'll never, never, never think again
Of love and me together. Not if I crawled
To wile him on with all sweet artifice
Of wooings and of shrinkings interchanged

Which many women do not shame to use,
And all men smile at, pleased to be deceived :
Not if I worshipped him with the fine fumes
Of delicate nice flattery some I know
Will offer to their idol, while his brain
Grows dizzy with the scent and pleasant mist :
Not if I played at him the pouts and scolds
And provocations of a mimic feud :
Not if I pleased him with an equal mind
To be convinced by arguments of his :
Not if I sang to tears for him, made mirth,
Were sad, wise, foolish, all for him alone :
Not if I lived my whole poor life for him :
No, not if it were so that I might die
To serve him something : he'd not love me yet,
He could not. When you're in a pleasant dream
And some one wakes you rudely, try your most,
You cannot dream again that selfsame dream.
'Tis over, gone. You cannot even think
Exactly how it went, with what quick turns.
You'll dream again, perhaps, as he, they say,
Dreams once more now, but not that dream again—
Oh never that.

      Kind Mary, talk to me
other things. No, let me tell you first,
you should too far scorn me), how it came
old love sprang sudden to a growth
my checking now.

Mary.   Dear, tell me all.
It comforts you to tell me. Do not fear
I cannot share it with you. I have now
So large a happiness that it is wide
To hold most sorrows—more than sorrow can.
I know that, I, who once had sorrow too,
And scorn you, darling? Do you think me then
So shallow-righteous that I can scorn grief
Because perhaps there went one drop of wrong
To tip its sting? Scorn you too for your love?
I know you have all pride a woman should
Of modesty. You talk to me because
It is, here in this twilight we were wont
To call "our time," like talking to yourself:
But I know well you have been hushed to him—
You'd not woo, you, if you could win him so.

    Lady B. Yet let me tell you. While my husband
       lived
In seeming strength I had a creeping fear
Would haunt my conscience like bad memories there,
As if, if he should die, I should perceive
A sense of freedom, and go lighter stepped,
And not be sad at all as I must seem.
But while I nursed him dying that was changed.
I did not feign the tenderness I shewed,
Nor wear my care for ornament. I seemed
To love him since he suffered. And I felt
That to *his* best he loved me. So I wept

Because we were to part with such an awe,
And he was scared at dying, *not* because
It seemed the wife's right way. And then, he dead,
The irretrievable strange going hence,
And something too the still dread show of death,
Struck me with such a sadness as made tears
A natural comfort to me, made the calm
Of one who has been grieving hush my life.
And while I still was sad a good kind soul—
If she had but grown dumb as well as deaf!—
Came with her cordial chatter. "So, my dear,
The widow's weeds put by. Well, quite time too :
You've worn them past the fashion for wives now.
I'm glad too; for my nephew's coming soon.
Don't think I did not know that naughty work—
You were too bad. But he could never bear
A word against you. Ah! he's true to you,
Like lovers in old times. You never heard
I think of that bad fever that he had
And raved of you long after you were wed.
Ah he raves now of you another way,
Poor boy. You'll not desert him now again."
I thought she knew. I had not seen him then
Since he had made me promise, but some months
Before my marriage, to be true to him,
And strong.—Strong! I who was too weak to stand
Against some breaths of anger and the stress
Of long persuasions and the paltry lure

Of being the great lady all ablow
With insolent wealth and fashion. Strong ! and I—
Why did he trust me ? He should have staid near,
If but to look at me the silent look
That made me feel my purpose confident
Because he trusted.

           Well, to tell my tale :
I played the cheat to him and to Sir Joyce :
Loved one and left him, did not love the other
And married him. But, foolishly enough,
It was the one I left who made complaint
As if I had been worth it. Laugh with me ;
How foolish men will be ! Aye you hold up
A warning finger. Well, I'll be sedate,
And pity my own sorrows decorously.
He was angry, had some bickering with Sir Joyce,
(They never told me what nor why), and so
They broke acquaintance and we never met.
How could I tell that the good cackler's talk
Was...what it was?

           Alas ! for many weeks
It chimed in like rich music when I thought,
Growing sweeter, sweeter, sweeter, day by day,
As never surely the good woman's words
Were heard in any ears before. I framed
My hopes, my fancies, purposes, to them,
And, since the time seemed long till he should come,
Spent my full heart in day-dreams.

Did I say,
A while ago, I'd dream here now with you
As we were wont? Ah! Mary, weariness
Can never dream. It sleeps, or is afire
With fever of a visionary toil
Over the trodden way that was so long.
I know no dreamings now.

Oh, foolish me!
I saw one bar, and only one. I thought
"He'd never take me with my clog of lands,
Houses, and shares, and so forth, which are mine
Because I was another man's. He's proud,
He will not be beholden to Sir Joyce."
And so among my dreams I saw the joy,
Of sacrificing what I once prized far
Beyond its worth, and still prized something well,
To him, to our new-blossomed love. And then
I fancied how he'd thank me, and forgive,
And praise me as in old days.

Well, we met.
I woke, at the first moment woke. He smiled,
And I could have shrieked, weeping out aloud,
But I smiled too. And bye and bye I tried
To fool myself a little: but 'twas vain.
We have talked often—always pleasantly,
Appropriately to the occasion too—
And I could hate myself who looked to him
For more than that. I heard a while ago

That he was new betrothed. I never asked
Was the news true or false. To me 'tis one.
Nothing could make me less to him than now,
Or more. To him I 'm—Talk of something else,
Of any thing but me. 'Tis your turn now.

    Mary. Well then of me. I 'll preach a little hope
Out of my simple life. Once, some years past,
I was betrothed—not yet so long ago
I could have told my tale more passionately,
With intricate vexed memories, have marked
The turns and changes and the subtle breaks,
Showing " I hoped thus " and " I sorrowed thus : "
But now I find so little to be told.
Whilst I was loving happily I learned
That I must love no more. I bade him wed
The mother of his child ; and that he did,
And has been worthier since. But, Eleanor,
I suffered. Nay I think it must be worse
Than one's own due remorse for wrong to find
Shame in you for the man you love. And I
Was heavy for the loss of love and hopes
That had been—ah we know what such hopes are.
I was so desolate for long. I would
That I could make you feel it; but myself
I cannot feel it now. The sun aglow,
Warm on my eyes, has dazzled them from sight
Of the clouds far floating backwards from the rent
It burst between them. Oh, dear Eleanor,

Never believe there is not happiness
Waiting you somewhere. I was helpless once,
And thought my life would limp on darkling, lost
In the clinging mist.
    Lady B.   And now you hope?
    Mary.   And now
I am happy, happy! Better too than that,
I make him happy—though that means the same.
    Lady B. You, Mary, you! I thought you'd mapped
        your life
In solitary busy spinsterhood.
    Mary. And he has quite remapped it. Did I
        know
There was a man like him out in the world
Without a woman loving him and loved?
And, dear, we seem well paired. We think alike
On most things, leaving but some needful points
For controversy lest we should be drowsed
By nodding constant Yes-es. We blend well
In tastes too. And, since we both have known a love
Which darkened into storm and wearied us
With tossing long unrest—for once he wooed
Some fickle beauty and believed he'd won,
And then she left him—since we have both known
That fret and fevering, 'tis well for us
To have, in our fixed trust, calm fearless rest.
    Lady B. Mary, you do not love him! No, you
        talk

Too soberly. You do not love him. No,
Not with your heart, the very life in you—
Less will not do. You must not ; no, you must not.
You shall not marry so. Oh ! if you guessed
What it will be to live as a wife lives
Beside a man who is not *all* to you !
All, all, I tell you.

  Mary.   Do you think we love
But with half hearts because our love to us
Is part of daily life, too known a thing
To praise or wonder at or analyse ?
We are so sure, so happy, love so well,
That we forget 'tis loving, as one breathes
Pure genial air and never notes one breathes.
Not love him ! Well, you'll see him presently,
You'll know how far from possible it were
For the woman who loves Lionel Ellerton
To love a little. You laugh, Eleanor,
With that strange bitter laugh of yours that rings
Always half like a cry to me who knew
The days when you were merry honestly.
You scorn such bright monotony, you'd have
A love like mountain-showers and sunlights mixed,
Dashes of anger but the love light still
Prompt to the eyes. But wait, dear Eleanor,
Till love worth you, that yet makes you more worth
That you may be worth it and him you love.
Comes, as it yet will come, must come, and then

3

You'll know what a rich thing my sunshine is,
My sunshine that makes beauty everywhere
Even upon the little cross black clouds
That cannot come athwart it but they change
And seem part of the sunshine.

Lady B.   Yes, I know,
I understand, no doubt you love him well,
And he loves you. For your sake I am glad.
But, tell me, dear, he never owned the name
Of his fickle ladylove, or let you guess?
I mean, is she repenting all forlorn,
A woe-begone thin spinster, mourning him?
Or is she plump and cosy, well to do,
With a fit husband, house, and chubby babes?
Or dead, more like—one way or other dead.

Mary.   We thought it best and right I should not
        know.
She is living, I might meet her, and 'twere hard
Not to be angry with her—though indeed
I have so much to thank her for. But then
She gave him pain he thought past bearing once
And shook his life to the very roots of it.

Lady B.   Dear, I am glad he loves you. It is
        good
To see you happy. I, whom no one loves,
Will pray you may be happy, both of you.
And I know something of your Lionel, know
He is a man well thought of, one I think

We can trust you to.

Mary. You know him?

Lady B. Why, he has
An uncle—or aunt's husband I should say—
And cousins—pretty too, the girls—who live
Not far from Boycott Hall. Sometimes he comes
To see them : I have met him there. They say
He's growing famous at the bar, rich too—
A very rising man. I give you joy.
A husband with both means and merit ! Why,
You must have sold your soul to have such luck,
Signed a red bond to Satan.

Mary. Well I think
We shall know how to cheat him. He'll not gain
Much by *our* marriage.

Lady B. Mary, promise me
You'll not betray me to your Lionel,
I would not have your lover know the trash
I've told you now. Weak baby trash enough,
But still my secret, Mary.

Mary. No indeed,
He'll never know it.

Lady B. No, he'll *never* know it.

Mary. Listen ! He's there. He thought he might
be kept
Until to-morrow. But I knew he'd come.

Lady B. Dear, go to him. I'm tired. I'll rest
to-night.

You'll say I'm tired—Or no, I'll follow you—
'Twill seem strange to your mother.   Presently
I'll follow.   Go to him.
    Mary.   Well if I must.   (*Exit Mary.*)
    Lady B. *Her* Lionel ! *Her* husband ! Oh my heart,
The pain in it ! *Her* lover ! If I wait
She'll say "We've Lady Boycott here," and then
The quick surprise may make him tell her more
Than she should know.   No, I must go to him,
Welcome him briskly, wear the cheerful face
Of pleasant meeting : he's my friend's betrothed,
And I must take him so.   'Twere easier
To ape indifference, dislike itself.
But I can play my part, and naturally,
And he'll not tell her, he'll be so at ease,
So careless of me.
              For she must not know.
I will not have her peace one moment stirred.
She'd pity me too kindly if she knew,
Be sad for me : I will not have her sad.
I love her for herself, and Lionel loves—
I could know nothing between hate and love,
I think, for any woman he would wed,
I must thank God I love her.   'Tis best so
And comforts me.
             Oh my rare smiling part !
My pretty cordial acting ! We shall be
A genial pair of friends.   We both love her,

And there's our bond. Oh! to be day by day
Talking and talking, smiling and smiling! Well
It will not last for ever. I have lied
In smiles and saying nothings prettily
To a worse purpose ere to-day.
                                        Ah me!
I thought that I was hopeless : now I know
I had a little foolish lingering hope.
'Tis strange I could! I knew so well the truth
That I was nothing to him.
                              Lionel,
I'm coming to you; I, not Eleanor:
She's gone, she's dead. But, as for Lady Boycott,
Perhaps you'll like her......she is Mary's friend.

Anno Domini 33.

I.

BARTIMÆUS.

BLUE happy sky, sweet lights of day,
　Round hills that lean against the air,
Clear grass blades shining in my way,
　How beautiful is everywhere!
I cannot see all that I would
　There is so much on every side,
　This glorious earth is very wide,
　And so much beauty to it given.
Dear Lord, the earth is wondrous good,
　It must be very like thy heaven.

I see! I see! Look the great field,
　A full bright lake of yellow ears
So sunlike that my eyes new healed
　See through a golden mist of tears!

Look, the broad fig-tree over-head,
  Oh cool green brightness through the leaves!
  What a fair web the spider weaves!
  Look where 'tis knit across the dock.
And who could find a richer red
  Than the flushed poppy's on that rock?

Beautiful! beautiful everywhere!
  Ah now I see that when I most
Moaned for lost sight in dim despair
  I but half felt what I had lost.
Oh! sight is happier than I knew:
  I had forgotten more, I find,
  What it was like not to be blind
  Than I believed. What! long ago
Was green so green and blue so blue?
  Did I laugh thus to see them so?

Oh darkness gone! oh dreary days!
  No human face, no world, no light!
Large darkness meeting my strained gaze,
  Vague darkness making sleep of sight!
And all around things wax and wane,
  And change and growth come over all,
  But the dull eyes see but their pall.
  And in the dark life seems so still;
Days come and go but you remain
  With vacant night and drowse your fill.

Oh, weariness of darkness gone,
  Broken as feverish last sleeps break
Because some sunbeam on us shone
  And we start up and are awake!
He was the sun that shone on me.
  He looked and I could feel the light,
  He spoke and once more I had sight,
  I saw the hills, I saw the sky,
I saw the sunlight on the tree—
  And I saw Him and did not die.

I saw Messiah's very face,
  My daylight seemed to break from Him,
And I stood rooted to the place,
  Trembling and cold in every limb.
And then I loved Him and was strong.
  He spoke it "Faith has made thee whole."
  Light in my eyes! Light in my soul!
  And I can love Him, and I see!
Oh Lord, the darkness was so long.
  Now I have sight—and I saw Thee!

Break into song, Oh! Zion, shout.
  Christ is among us, Christ the Light.
Darkness is gone, and sin, and doubt.
  Oh golden time! the blind have sight.

Light, light is on us, there is day.
From the glad earth a ringing voice
Bounds through my heart "Rejoice, rejoice,"
Behold the day-spring from on high.
Rejoice the night has passed away,
Jesus of Nazareth comes by.

Anno Domini 33.

II.

JUDAS.

AYE, what is it to them? They are content.
He's dead. No shrinking now at words of his
Scorning them, aye and what they hated more,
Teaching them, they the teachers. He had eyes
That saw too far through hearts, and so he's dead.
And what is it to them if I, the tool
Who did their wickedness at a low price,
Am God-accursed? No, they'll not even waste
A little cheap hypocrisy—no praise
For serving Israel's Lord, no promises
Of honour from my nation, no pretence
Of freeing me from blood-guilt—all that's past.
"What's that to us? Look to it thou thyself."
    They gathered up my coins, though. All men love
The shining of good monies. How they'll mock:

"We drove that bargain well, at least. The fool!
To sell his Master on such easy terms,
And his own soul too—though what's that to us?
And then to toss us back the price again
As if that could change matters."

                  No, I'll have
My money back: they shall not profit so.
Rather the sea shall have it. The full sea
Will take it greedily, as a man takes,
And never look the fuller. But I doubt—
Not *doubt*, I *know* some horrible strange chance
Would kill me if I took it in my hands.
I dare not touch it. Let them keep it then,
And take the curse with it.

                The price of blood!
And who's? But He, how could he die indeed?
He could not with our death. Not if he was
Whom I at times believed him, Whom he said.
And if he said it falsely then 'twas fit
His dupes should be unduped—the priests urged that.
I could not go amiss: if he were Christ,
His glory would burst forth and dazzle earth,
Wake up our Zion, scare the Romans hence;
And if not Christ, why then the dread of death
Would make him speak plain words of what he was,
And be set free forgiven.

                But he'd bate
No jot, no tittle, would be only Christ.

And yet he died.   He could not have been Christ.
And then what was he?

                When I followed him,
The first great day he came among our hills
And talked of love and truth, he who was both
Whatever else he was, I knew at once
That God had sent him to us, and I thought
I felt God's voice bid me go forth with him.
Who was it sent me with him?   Satan then
That I might murder him?

                     That black slow cloud,
Heavy on Calvary, looks ghastly now—
He might be in it, He, my lord, my friend.
If His face looked on me I should fall dead
Even if it should seem no more than man's.
I go in dread of that, and every sound
Has something of his voice in it.   There's talk
As if he should appear still on the earth,
Stand life-like near the living, speak to them—
Great God!—nay 'tis my folly.   That long sigh
Of wind among the olives is not new
That it should startle me.   I've often sat
And listened to it when the night came on
With its shrill breezy rustlings like the sea
We'd hear at home plashing on pebbly shores
Far from us, and it always seemed to me
To make me quieter as His voice did.
His voice!   How every thought comes back to Him!

Can I know nothing then but this one man,
Him crucified? Why I have other friends—
No I mean *had*. I lost my natural friends
When I cast in my lot with him they thought
A devil's preacher sent to cozen us
With holy maxims, lost them for his sake,
Father and brother, yes my mother too,
Teachers and comrades and familiar guests,
They turned and loathed me. And my new friends
     now,
I am a leper to them, one cast out
Past mercy from them. Would there one of them
Look upon me if I should crawl to him,
Grovel beneath his feet crying "Oh man,
Touch me that I may feel I am a man.
Touch with thine hand?" Would Peter, or would
     James,
Or even sweet-tongued John? Would I forgive
If one of them had done the accursed deed?
No there's not one in all the world to speak
A praying word for me, not even to say
"Let him but die and never wake from death
Let him not know the name or face of God
Nor Jesus whom he slew; let him but die
As the beast dies, and rot as the dead tree,
And be no more." Himself was merciful,
But no mere men would be thus merciful:
They'd say "No, let him live on with the sense

Of darkness round him and of some one near—
As if a murderer dragged the corpse with him
And shivered sickly lest it should arise
And shrivel him with dreadful ghostly looks,
Alive with awful life. Yes, let him breathe
With the sharp gasps of some mad hunted thing
When none pursue. Let him cry out aloud
With anguish, and not know how to repent.
Let him go agonized with doubt, and know
Doubt and belief make no more now for him
Than for dumb dogs. Only let him not die
And fall asleep." Yes none will say " His pain
Is more than he can bear."

Where Jesus was
None could be friendless, none despair : and now—
My name is blotted from among the names
Of the living, there is no man says to me
"Alas my brother!" There is no God for me
Who heareth prayer. I only in the world
Have not a God to cry to. Who is God
But He who sent us Christ? And who is Christ
But Jesus the Nazarene, Jesus who had
The Godhead in him? Die, thou lost one, die !
I know him now and tremble, know Him now
Whom I believed in vaguely, whom I sold !
How should I pray? "Jehovah whose own Son,
A very part of thee, I did to death,
Be very gracious to me for His sake ?"

Aye so, He said prayer should be in his name,
And taught us how to use it. Properly
'Twould fit my lips—His name a plea for me !
Would God that Baal had a life in him
And could at least do harm. I'd pray to him
" Baal, for love of my great sin, do thou
Give me kind nothingness, make me a thing
Like thy block image, soulless, ignorant
Of light and darkness and of any thought."
" Baal," I'd say, "fall on me, batter me
To piecemeal rubbish, and drag down my soul
To thy void chaos where 'twill rot with thee,
To thy void chaos where God will not come,
Nor Jesus."
        Did my heart leap to him once,
Our holy Master? Surely it did once.
I left my home, even as the others left,
Left all my worldly goods to follow him,
Even as the others, bore with scoffs and taunts,
And tender sad reproach more hard to bear.
I loved the holiness he taught, I loved
The love, I loved the glorious saintly scorn
Of all things tyrannous and cunning, loved
The pitying tenderness for all things weak.
And then his talk stirred longings in my heart
For freer breath than we draw now, strong days
Rid of the hindering trammels we have now,
Justice and mercy in our streets, rich peace,

And God to rule and judge us as of old.
I thought the looked-for King was come in Him,
And he would so deliver us. I looked
To see the Romans scattered, fleeing hence,
Calling in terror on their idle gods,
Before avenging Israel. I looked
To have our Zion sing the song of praise,
And the hills laugh with golden harvests thick
Up to their brows, and the green valleys ring
With singing of full rivers through the fields,
Because the great Messiah King was come
With spoils in His right-hand of all our foes
And blessings for the people. But he seemed
To bow the neck to Cæsar patiently
And care for no deliverance. Poverty
Was the first blessing that he offered us
To make the world a kind one. And we saw,
We who were watching for his cry to sound
"Now Israel to your tents," we who believed
We should be leaders under him and lords,
To have the people honour us, and live
In our ceiled palaces among the tribes
Content and prospering around us, saw
He would but teach submission to the yoke,
Saw we were only chosen to be poor
More than all others, meaner, more despised,
Servants of servants, we. And many turned,
And saw his face no more. But I remained,

I loved his teaching though it angered me,
I saw the greatness of it.

                     Would to God
I too had left him !

                  Why did they all smile
With mocking eyes, that day when I was vexed
To see the spikenard wasted ?. If they had had
The wisdom to be secret of their thoughts
And somewhat less discerning, those prompt priests
With their shrewd chaffering might perhaps have had
No bargain out of me—I'd said them nay
To more before that time, and to my thought
They'd ceased to look to me for any help.
Why did the others ´chafe me ? If the purse
Had now and then, 'twas rarely, furnished me
A secret pittance to supply the needs
And hide the shame of the poor squalid life
I led with sick dislike, had I not lost
The promise of good days ? Had I not lost
My chance of growing gains, my handicraft
To earn me something more ·than beggar's fare ?
Did I not always with my nicest skill,
Such as not one of them could reach, swell out
Our wretched means and make two pence like three ?
Why, but by that, I gave more than I took,
Threefold and fourfold. Yes the brethren might
Have spared their smiles. How hot they made my
      heart !

I hated them.

    And then His grave sad look!
He saw too far into men's hearts. What man
Can live with one who knows him at his worst?
It makes him have no best. I could not bear
Their scorn, His knowing. I would show them all
I had some power—aye and I had a purse
Besides their bag to draw from. In my haste
I went—and afterwards it seemed too late.
I know not how, the priests can argue well,
If they pay smally. And the time was short;
I never seemed to have the space to think,
Till I awoke, and *knew*.

     The time was short.
He saw too far into men's hearts: he knew
The purpose dizzying mine. Aye, there was need
To hasten its fulfilment. Could I wait
And nurse it while he watched me? "What thou doest
Do quickly." And I did not dare to ask
A meaning for it. He knew me. And I fled
Out from his presence. What had it served then
To lag and waver, and perchance repent?
He knew me.

    Jesus is dead, is dead. Go to,
The very devils, sure, must mourn for that;
For I mourn. Jesus is dead, who looked on me
As if he loved me though he knew me. Dead!
I never thought they'd kill him. Dead, I say.

Out on you priests with your false glozing tongues,
Liars and murderers. Aye shoot your lips,
Look with your triumphing cold sidelong looks,
Take your full ease again, you've had your way.
There's one who could have saved the world from
      death
Sickness and sin and weepings, dead through you.
What's that to you? There's one, your purchased
      wretch,
Mad with the worst guilt the foul world has known,
His very prayer made sin. What's that to you?
You're very pious, you observe the law,
You have no blood-gouts on your fringe, you've caught
No unclean taint by touching death too near,
You only planned and plotted, you are pure.
You kept the high-day too, the cross was bare
When the sun set on the mere labouring day.
Oh zealous saintly rulers! holy men!
But I am only a poor common man,
And ignorant, and I must bear the curse
Of generations of lost death-struck men
Who'll cry "One came to save us, Jesus came,
But Judas took him from us." If I die
Or if I live the cry will still ring out
And shiver through and through me worse than pain—
"The world is lost, lost, left a prey to death
For ever and for ever since Christ died."
Oh me accursed! the dead shall have their graves

For ever, and the living have no hope,
Israel have no Messiah! Will not earth
Cover me in her Hades out of sight
Of all these men whose souls I have destroyed?
I've done so much for death can I not die
Body and soul, body and soul, like all;
Body and soul out of the sight of death,
That I have made the Master of the world;
Out of the sight of life and death; henceforth
Both misery to every soul that breathes?
Why I can die. Why surely I can die
Like other men. I only of the world
To have the perfect life all were to have—
And find it perfect anguish! That might be:
'Twere a rare vengeance on me, well assigned.
But death is for us all. I can have death
I'll think of it—body and soul asleep!

𝕬𝖓𝖓𝖔 𝕯𝖔𝖒𝖎𝖓𝖎 33.

III.

PILATE.

Pilate. Foolishness! foolishness! Fye, you weary
    me.
You are so small, you women, cannot peep
Over the fence next to you; so self-willed,
You'll not trust other's eyes who see a world
Stretched out beyond it. "Dearest" says the man,
"I see some certain hills and valleys there;
I'll draw them in my picture of the world."
"Not so" the woman says, "there's nothing more
Than this green yard we stand in. Map it out
And that's the world." And so she'll make her roads
Run straight to little points within the hedge,
And never thinks there may be curves to take
To reach great points outside.
    Procla.   And does that mean

A woman thinks a judge is to·be just,
And a man thinks a judge is to resolve
What policy were spoiled if he were just?
  Pilate. It means a man, a ruler as I am,
Must look beyond the moment, must allay
Justice with prudence. Innocence is much
To save a man, but is not everything
Where a whole province is at stake for Rome.
How many lives think you had cost this life
Refused to these hot zealots? In one word
Sum up the answer—war. You tender soul
Who weep so for this one man dead, what tears,
What cataracts of tears would wear the sight
Out of your frightened eyes if I had been,
What by the Gods I longed to be, mere just,
Had, starving them of their sweet blood-draught,
        roused
The wild dog lurking in each several man
Of your dear Jews, these stubborn sullen Jews
Who are ready any moment to spring up
And flesh their teeth in Roman throats? Aye, think—
Bloody rebellion loosed; the ready cry
"Insult to Moses' law" howled through the land,
Maddening these tiger tribes; the Roman sway
Tottering and rent as by an earthquake's throes;
Our Romans hacked and maimed and trampled, snared
In ambushes and onslaughts in the dark.
And then the vengeance! these your hero Jews,

Whose myths and hymns so take you, trodden out
Like reptiles underneath the heel; not one,
But hundreds, crucified; rapine and fire
And slaying everywhere.   Then, bye and bye,
The province settled in an angry peace,
Half our Jews dead, the other half grown dumb
For utter fear, and Rome supreme again,
Cæsar bethinks him whence the mischief came:
"Our procurator—What! to save one man
Who preached, he thought, a fine philosophy
He put a slight upon the famous law
He was bidden touch so gingerly, and set
The land in that fierce uproar!   Call him home
And let him answer it."   You'd blame me then
In sadder fashion, Procla.   Aye, I know
You women do it.   Always 'tis a fault,
Never an evil fortune.   A man dies,
You're wretched, but you tell him while he dies
It was his fault.

    Procla.   Alas! Have I deserved
This bitterness?

    Pilate.   Because you harp and harp
On one cross theme—that necessary death.
You know it vexed me sharply.   Let me be.
The past is past, the dead are dead, and groans
And "would I had not"s will not make not done
That which was not done scarce a minute back.
Fate's self can never say "the past is not,"

Only the coming swerves for fate or gods,
And how can a man's sorrow touch it then?

   Procla. He may find good from sorrow for ill
     deeds.

   Pilate. What good? Will sorrow lengthen a man's
     days

Or give him wealth or triumphs? Sorrow eats
Into the heart like a wasp into the fruit,
Eats up the pith within you, leaves you, like
The Dead Sea dust fruits, proper to the sight
For customary use, but inwardly
Unserviceable ashes. Do you think
I've vexed Apollo or some fire-breathed God
Who'll dart a plague on me unless I bend
And offer hecatombs? No, no, the wrong
Is but against my nature and the man
Who died not having sinned; so there is none,
Nor God, nor man, to whom I can atone.
Nor see I how my sorrowing would help.

   Procla. I know it. Yet, if Jesus were divine—
   Pilate. What then, you Nazarene?
   Procla.   Why then 'twould be
As if you had vexed Apollo. You would bring
A sacrifice to make his anger cease.

   Pilate. My child, this Jesus, if he *were* divine,
Was a philosopher. Such would not snuff
Our reeking altar smokes with much delight.
What sacrifice could *he* have?

Procla.   I have heard
He used to say the sacrifice to him
Was sorrow for ill-doing
    Pilate.   Said he that?
If a poet now could have his pick of Gods
To put in heaven, he'd make him one for that.
My Procla, I have heard of many things
Most noble and most touching that man taught,
And I believe that he, though of mean state,
Not tutored as I think in subtle lore
Of the wise Greeks nor of our reasoning schools,
Would yet have left his stamp upon the world
As deep as any sage's, would have raised
A school of teachers of the highest flight
Who might perhaps have learned for us some things
We vaguely yearn to know of, found perhaps
Something to take for real and hold fast
In the confusion of philosophies
And shifting dulled traditions of our Gods
Who let us wander on and make no sign—
For what are we to them or they to us?
Something at least to take for starting point
Amid the coil of labyrinths that twist
And fret and cross and bring us back again
To where we were, the labyrinths that seem
To wreath and puzzle round a gaping void
Where truth, we're told, should be,—a starting point
To find the clue from, and perhaps the goal....

Which our philosophers put out of count,
As if the work was to make labyrinths,
More than we have, and see where they might end.
For him, he seemed, if he had not seen truth,
At least to think he had; and that is much.
And if I *could* have saved him, but for this
That he might reason with me, I had done it.
And I, whom the Jews call a cruel man,
At least love justice as a Roman should,
And that man's innocence, (I tell you this
That you may cease to make my trouble worse),
Weighs on me like my guilt, though I indeed
Absolve myself from share in dooming him.
But there was no way left; you know I tried
To save him and I failed. No more of this.
Now never vex me with his name again,
Unless you'd have me loathe you as I loathe
The murderous Jews who dragged their victim from
  me
By threats of Cæsar.
 Procla.   No, you'll love me still.
I will not fret you, you are grieved enough.
But you'll have his name forced upon you yet—
They say he's risen.
 Pilate.   Pretty simpleton,
You look as awestruck, draw your breath as quick
As if you were no wiser than the geese
That cackle in the back lanes of all towns.

Risen, my baby! I have heard this talk.
And do you think death but an actor's mask
To be thrown off and there's the man alive?
I would he could be risen. I should laugh
To˙ see the Jews' scared faces. More than that
I should be thankful, sleep more easily;
And you'd smile all the sweeter. But the dead
Lie stark and helpless, then rot into earth,
And there's an end. That's the deep sadness, child,
Which all our hearts, outface it as we will,
Faint at and whimper at through all our thoughts,
That the dead are really dead and not asleep,
And so there is no rising. Nay indeed
If they should rise, what body could they wear?
Is there not loathsome mildewing decay
That eats the putrid flesh? My fond fair wife,
Let us take life as softly as we can
So hard a toil, and gild it with all joys,
And not nurse sorrow on it, as you'd do,
Because of evil chances; for so soon
As it is given us foul death begins
To nibble at it, and one day he gnaws
The heartstrings and we go back to the earth,
And there's nor joy nor sorrow nor fond hope,
For we are nothing.
    Procla.   Do you think indeed
There is no soul?
    Pilate.   I know there is a soul,

Since there's a body and the body moves
And feels and breathes, though 'tis such reeking dung
When something's gone, the something that is soul.
But that dies first, gasps into nothingness,
And after that the body dies and fats
The earth it came of. Nay, if the soul lived
As part of the great breath we call the air
And so a part of life and every life,
What life were that to us to call it ours?
We die, my Procla, and to die is death.

    Procla. Those Jewish wondrous writings which I
      love
And you call glorious phantasies allow
Another sense to death—which one should come
To show men plainly, so that none should die.
Oh husband, if this Jesus were the man
Or god who was to show it!

    Pilate.   Aye, indeed
That were a parlous loss! But they can hope
And dream without a teacher, and what more
Could any teach them than to hope and dream?
And now, dear Procla, leave me, I have work,
Letters and long reports to write for Rome.
Go to your tapestries—a fitter use,
And fairer, for your wits than these sad thoughts
Which, saddening us, may make us sooner die,
But cannot soften death. Go dear.

    Procla.   I go.

But as for tapestries, the needle flies
And thought flies quicker. Sorrow will not die
Upon the needle's point. Good bye awhile.
    Pilate. Good bye, be merry, and forget this talk.
                        (*Exit Procla.*)
Aye, so one says forget. She may forget:
Women are but bird-minded, flying quick
And eager from one tree-perch to the next,
And sometimes lighting on a thorny bough,
By chance, but not for long. A day or two
And she'll forget the prophet, be content
With her dear Jewish legends. But, for me,
Her sobbings and her talk will vex me, long
'Past her remembering them. I'm strangely moved!
Indeed these several days I have not lost
The sense of shame that shook me when he looked
With quiet eyes at me, standing condemned
By my allowance. Wonderful weird man!
If gods indeed would take men's shapes, I'd say
I saw the God in him. ' It is past thought
That any, even haters like the Jews,
Could hate him. Well they did and murdered him.
But I am guiltless of his blood. I went
To the utmost verge of prudence—nay, beyond—
To check the infuriate mob. Yes, by the gods,
No light task 'twould have been to clear myself
For my part in the mischief, if there'd grown
A riot from the trial, and that seemed like

Before I yielded.   They are hard at Rome
On luckless governors.   Aye, aye, my Jews
Had made a rare case of it: for the man,
Though to our Roman sense most innocent
Of all save too much wisdom for their wits,
Was doubtless somewhere tangled in the toils
Of their fastidious laws.   Why, he had washed
At the wrong time—or had not washed, which was
        it?
He said the Scribes were pedants and the priests
Rank hypocrites...which only we may say,
And which we're bidden not say to the Jews;
He told the mob their God was, after all,
More than their Moses; and, most heinous sin,
He healed their sick on sabbaths.   By their law
He ought to die; their rulers urged that loud.
Never let any say I was unjust.
"The Son of God" he took for name, they said.
Belike one of their Syriac metaphors
Which, like hot-tempered kestrels, overfly
The quarry aimed at.   But, if he did mean
To boast a mystic kindred with some source
Of life and thought divinely different
From the every-day plain sires who made our lives,
I'd never mock his claim until I knew
Its secret import.   Not if the title was
Of his own taking.   If the sheepish herds,
That flock around each new teacher, all asweat

With running and jostling for the nearest place,
To stare and wonder what he means and cry
"Oh the rare teacher !" till the next one comes,
So dubbed him, why, 'tis but the ancient tale :
The multitude, self-conscious, thinks a man
Must be a fool and base, and when it finds
One who is neither, or at least not both,
Is sure by that his father is a god,
Or he's a god himself, or going to be.
But Jesus if he said I am the Son
Of a divine one, or of the One God,
Implied some esoteric subtlety
With a great import—for I looked on him
And heard him speak, and his was no crazed soul,
Fired from its own dank heat like ill-housed ricks ;
And no impostor, sane, would in such stead
Have kept so obstinate a courage.
                                Truth !
He claimed to know truth, which no man yet knew.
Was that his meaning?   Truth is real life,
Such as the gods might have, and he had reached
To truth and so was as One near the gods,
Or near the great One God—which possibly
Is but a name of life.
                        But why waste thought
To beat out the philosophy or creed
He would have taught, from the disfiguring husks
Rough rumour gives as grain?   The man is dead ;

Guilty or innocent, wise or possessed,
He sleeps the silent sleep which ends all hope,
And we may bawl our questions at his door,
He'll make no answer.   Dead philosophers
Are just as useful to the living world'
As are dead lions, or dead rats...they help
To make good soil.   As for the coins they leave,
Of thought, for us to heir, why, ninety-nine
Out of each hundred stamp their own images
On all their dies, and so the coins mean nought,
Save to disciples who will let them pass
As money 'twixt themselves, still bickering,
The while, about their values.   If by chance
We take the mint of one man for some worth,
Then in a trice we're rich with counterfeits
Yielding base metal to the assayer's tests.
Let the sage live and give us his own gold,
That's something : we are all disciples then
After a fashion.   For at least we're sure
That what we hear him speak he speaks—or thus,
The sounds he makes have such results on ears
Which are our own, and so we say we're sure,
Though in true sense we're sure of nothing.

                                        Aye,
We're sure of nothing.   That's the wretched void
Which makes all thinking sad and like the wind
That with much blustering breaks itself a way
And passes on to nowhere.   We live now,

And life means a great hurrying on to death;
And then we die and death means nothingness;
And weep, or scoff, or reason at it, still
Two facts so bald as these are all we have
For fruit of all our pains, and those we had
Taking no pains at all. All other things,
As how we live, and why, and whence, remain
A fretting mystery. Like shipwrecked men
We try to float upon a sea of doubts:
We'd swim for shore if there were any shore,
But the only ground at hand to give us rest
Is the loathed home of dead things underneath.

This Jesus now—how strangely he has seized
Upon my mind! I cannot lose the sense
Of his sad look fixed on me sovereign
With patient high rebuke—he seemed to wear
A quiet on him, as if he *did* rest,
As if he somehow would have given rest
To those who learned of him. But he is dead;
And I half feel as if in killing him
They had refused the last hope of the world
For any comfort in the heavy gloom
That death and doubt throw on it. *They!* say *we*.
I am accomplice; gloze it as I will
With fair and true excuses, in my heart
It rankles a great shame and bitterness.
I killed him, I, the unjust and coward judge
Who cringed before the passion of a mob

5

And was their tool. Gods! 'twas a hideous deed,
A dastardly foul deed, to let him die.
I'm sick at it, I'm weary like a man
Who carries crimes on him he dares not name
Even to his next and dearest lest they'd turn
And loathe him. Every creeping silent hour
Since I beheld him haled forth to the cross
Has dragged an age of thought with it, and what
I know not how to name except as dread.

And yet what do I dread? But more and more,
Like a poor baby shuddering in the dark
And peopling loneliness with awful shades,
I feel as if I could not be alone
Because I tremble. Somewhere there must be
A terror near, or why should I be scared?
There's all my reasoning. The baby cries,
And some one helps it, lights it safe to bed.
The man must hold his peace, or they'll say "mad"
And chain and lash him long before he's mad
With trying to make out his bugbear's shape.

Nay I'll not peer for mine. I could not bear
Poor Procla's fancies and I sent her hence,
To be in peace, but my own fancies are
Like monster shadows, hers thrown hideously
On lurid mists. What! can I never now
Trust myself with myself? Must there still come
This madman's mood upon me, as if guilt
Were more than man can bear who yet bears death

With pleasantness if any one be near
To give him honour for it?

                     Ah! they say
Through all his anguish he would still look down
With an ineffable strange pitying,
As if 'twas those below who died, not he;
They say through all he—nay, no more of this.
The crime sits hard enough on my wrung mind
Without these useless broodings to swell out
Its vampire bulk. I know too certainly
I shall be haunted with it all my days,
As if the Furies clung to me. But I
Refuse the guilt, I did not will the doom;
Let the Jews look to it, they took his death
On them and on their children.

                    But if aught
Could purify me I'd give this right hand
The water should have cleansed from that just blood,
To purchase that redemption.

                  Well, 'tis naught.
To weep past evil is a vainer thing
Than to shake drops of dew upon the fire.
I'll think no more of it—were't possible
I'd never think again. There's much to do,
These letters should be sent to Rome at once.

Anno Domini 33.

IV.

THE WALK TO EMMAUS.

Cleopas. I cannot see to reason, 'tis as if
I walked amid a cloud and saw all blurred
Through its slow hazes, nothing certain shaped.
What this portends I guess not. But 'tis strange.
   The other Disciple. Most strange indeed! The
        closing stone roll'd back
By stealth! the body stolen from the tomb!
Think you the rulers have done this, for fear
His tomb should be a sacred place for us
Who loved him, and the fickle people, moved
With memory of his great signs and words,
Might come and touch his tomb with reverence,
And build about it a great monument
To honour him to all the future days,
A prophet, yea and more?

Cleopas.   Nay but they said,
The women, they had looked upon and heard
A vision of great angels.
    The other.   Idle tales.
Alas! they have been weeping now so long,
They go distraught for sorrow.   One of them
Had a sick fancy, and the rest, all scared
And horror-struck because the dead was gone,
Believed her ravings, and came huddling back,
Breathless like children who have news to tell
And could not wait to see if it were true
Lest some one else should tell it first.   Their words
Seemed to the Apostles idle tales, and they
Know more than we.
    Cleopas.   But then the Lord is gone.
    The other.   Yes they have taken him.   Would we
        but knew
Where they have laid him!   Will they wreak their
        hate
Even on the dead?   Oh cruel! could they not
Have left us so much comfort as there is
To weep outside a grave?
    Cleopas.   And yet he talked
Of rising.
    The other.   Dost thou think it?   Did that mean
That he should rise his own same self again?
    Cleopas. Alas who knows?   He shewed us many
        things

Which we perceived but dimly, for weak eyes
Wink at the light and see it in a haze.
We cannot tell.　He said he was the life,
Yet he saw death.　He came to be our light,
And we grope in the darkness, crying out
To know which way we tend, and none replies,
Nor takes our hand to set us in the path.
　　The other.　Aye, we may weep.　We seemed to
　　　　have a hope
For Israel and for us.　And lo ! the strength
Of Satan has been stronger than Christ's strength.
We are given over to our sins and death,
God will not pity us.　He has looked down　·
On Israel's stubbornness, and turns aside
His purposed blessing from us.　Jesus came
And said " Be happy, be the sons of God."
And Israel answered " Nay, but we will have
The yoke that is too heavy and the pain
That is too sharp.　We will not come to thee
For life, but we will live *our* life and die."
And Israel answered " Nay but thy sweet words
Are bitter in our ears because of sin.
Depart from us, be dumb among the dead."
And so they slew him.　Oh ! our Master slain
With the transgressors !　And the promise given
For ages and for ages, Israel's hope
And consolation, marred in the very hour
Of its fulfilment !　Now shall men drudge on

For ever in the same unhopeful round,
Sadder than sunless days, for Christ is slain
Who was the Sun of lives.

                               Cleopas. So after all
Thou too continuest sure he is the Christ.
    The other. We who have known him, know he
        was the Christ
Because he told us so. In all this doubt
We will not doubt of that. But, woe is me
For our lost hope! Christ should have ruled the world.
    Cleopas. Therefore it seems to me death cannot have
Dominion over him.
    The other.   It should be so.
But he is dead.
    Cleopas.   Yet if the angels spake
"Why will ye seek the living with the dead?
He is not here."
    The other.   Alas! my Cleopas,
We saw him die.
    Cleopas.   There is another life.
    The other. Yes, some dim other life which was a
        sleep
Until Messiah came...then should be life.
But he has come, and now what is that life?
For whom do the sleepers wait?
    Cleopas.   My brother, hear.
I am not subtle, cannot gather up
The several threads of counter prophecies

And show them crossing but as woof and warp,
But I trust God and Jesus whom he sent,
Whom we call Lord.   God shall save Israel
From all their sins: the promise was set forth
In many signs and many various words,
And came scarce a day later to the world
Than sin itself, which the serpent taught the world.
The promise was because of sins.   Shall then
The father of all sins, who is the serpent,
Be master of the world through Israel's sin
Against the promise?   Can men thwart God's will?
Jesus also himself declared to us
We should be comforted.   How comforted,
If he sleep carelessly among the dead,
And the hope die with him?   Since Christ is come
It must be that the promise is fulfilled,
And is fulfilled in him?

 The other.   Fulfilled?   But how?
 Cleopas.   I know not.   Oh, my brother, we *must*
   weep,
And the tears darken out the light.
 The other.   We weep
Because the light is gone.
 Cleopas.   Oh Jesus, Lord,   •
Light out of Heaven, our glory and our love,
Thou art gone from us.   Gone! Oh! can the dead
Hear thee and love thee as the living once?
Why then the dead are living, we are dead.

Let us live with thee Lord among the dead.
Alas! I am a blind man crying out
For sight, and know not if my eyes would wake
On only heavy darkness of the night
Or if there's day upon the earth.
 The other.   Alas!
Can day give any comfort to the blind?
And, Jesus gone, we every one are blind,
With none to heal us. Oh our light! our life!
Thou gone we are blind, we are dead. Oh Cleopas,
Had God forsaken him?
 Cleopas.   Oh no, no, no.
It could not be. Our Christ! the Son of God!
 The other. The Son of God, as we believe, God's
   Own,
A very part of God. And yet he died
Even as a man dies whose life is wind.
And where then is our hope?
 Cleopas.   Woe, woe, is me!
Is then our hope made vanity? Is life
The way to death? Nothing but the way to death?
Shall the world lie in darkness to the end
And desolate?

AND JESUS HIMSELF DREW NEAR.

THE OLD YEAR OUT AND THE NEW YEAR IN.

RING then, ring loudly, merry midnight bells,
  Peal the new lord of days blithe welcoming—
What though your sweet-scaled tones be also knells,

Be knells the while for the old fallen king
  Resting his dying head upon the snow?
Ring out the old year, for the new year ring.

Mock him with laughing voices, bid him go;
  Let him make haste to rest among the dead,
He is no more a lord for life to know.

Ring in the coming year; *his* power has fled,
  He has no blessing and no sorrow more.
Ah well; yet should no tear for him be shed?

Surely some gift of good to men he bore,
  He too was greeted as an honoured guest;
Ah fickle! do we joy his reign is o'er?

Should we so vex him, as he sinks to rest,
  Greeting with glad acclaim his passing sigh?
He droops into his grave unmourned, unblest;

With dying ears he hears the joyous cry
  That bids his rival take his crown and reign;
The mirth of music and of songs laughs by;

He hears men merry at his dying pain,
  "He breathes his last, laugh him a gay good-bye."—
And yet he did not live with us in vain.

But what is this to me? Well, let him die.
  Did he bring any joy or good to me?
He taught me tears, shall tears now flood mine eye?

But I among the rest make jubilee,
  (Here in the midnight, sitting all alone,
Far in my heart from any thought of glee),

And, triumphing to see him overthrown,
  I say "Yes die, make haste to thy far flight,
Let the new days reap that which thou hast sown."

For thou hast sown; and if thy stormful might
  Has crushed the buddings of the former years,
Ah well! their fields of promise were too bright,

Too bright—oh! childish folly of vain tears,
　To weep for weeds which were no more than fair,
And dwarfed the fulness of the golden ears!—

Too bright with cornflowers and the crimson flare
　Of idle poppies, and with purpled chains
Of trailing vetch too frail its weight to bear.

Well, thou hast broken them with thy strong rains
　And buried them to death beneath thy snows—
What though with them have sunk the swelling grains?

For nought can perish quite; the crimson glows
　Will be more faint, the purples pale away,
But harvest wealth will wave in closer rows.

The buried blooms give life from their decay,
　And strength and fulness to the aftergrowth,
Out from their graves it climbs to perfect day.

So comes a richer fruit. Why am I wroth
　With thee, old year? And yet I am content:
Now in that thought, now this, and doubting both.

I say "Haste hence; I joy thy life is spent,
　I shall breathe freer when thy reign is o'er;
Let the young lord of hopes make his ascent."

I say "Oh dying year, my heart is sore
   For thee who hast become a part of me,
I grieve that I shall see thy face no more."

And all the while the death-chills creep o'er thee
   Lying on thy cold couch 'mid snow and rain ;
A moment now, and thou hast ceased to be.

Hark ! hark ! the music of the merry chime !
   The King is dead ! God's blessing on the King !
Welcome with gladness this new King of Time.

Oh merry midnight bells, ring blithely, ring,
   Wake with your breathless peal the startled night,
High in your belfry in mad frolic swing.

Laugh out again, sweet music and delight,
   In happy homes a moment hushed to hear
The midnight strokes boom out the old year's flight.

See, he is gone for ever, the old year,
   Why should we vex our hearts with sad farewells ?
Let the dead sleep, bare not his shrouded bier.

Ring on, ring yet more gladly, merry bells,
   Peal the new lord of days glad welcoming—
What though your happy chimes be also knells ?

IN THE STORM.

A WILD rough night: and through the gloomy grey
　　One sees the blackness of the headland grow,
One sees the whiteness of the upflung spray,
　　The whiteness of the breakers down below.

A wild wild night: and on the shingly rim
　　The furious sea-surge roars and frets and' rives;
And far away those black specks, growing dim,
　　Are tossing with their freights of human lives.

And all the while upon the silent height
　　The strong white star, beneath the starless sky,
Shines through the dimness of the troubled night,
　　Shines motionless while the vexed winds hoot by.

Oh! steadfast light, across dark miles of sea
　　How many straining eyes whence sleep is chased
Are watching through the midnight storm for thee
　　Large glimmering through the haze to the grey waste!

And in the night, fond mothers, scared awake,
    And lonely wives, pushing the blind aside,
See thee and bless thee for their sailor's sake,
    And thank God thou art there, the dear ship's guide.

Oh! strong calm star, so watching night by night,
    And hour by hour, when storm-winds are astir,
They find thee changeless with thy patient light,
    A beacon to the sea-tossed wanderer.

Oh strong and patient! Once upon my life
    Shone such a star, and, when the trouble wave
Reached me and I grew faint with tempest strife,
    Through all I saw that hope-star and was brave.

Oh my lost star! my star that was to me
    Instead of sunlight that the happy know!
Oh weary way upon life's trackless sea!
    And through the gloom there shines no beacon glow.

NEVER AGAIN.

NEVER again. This shivering rose, that sees
Its dwindled blossoms droop and fall to earth
Before the chillness of the Autumn rain,
Will bud next summer with more fair than these—
But when have love's waned smiles a second birth?
        Never again, Never again.

Never again. Oh dearest do you know
All the long mournfulness of such a word?
And even you who smile now on my pain
May seek some day for love lost long ago
And sigh to the long echo faintly heard
          Never again, Never again.

Never again. The love we break to-day
May linger in my heart unto the last;
And even with you some memory must remain,
But ah! no more. The sunlight died away
Will wake again, but never wakes the past—
          Never again, Never again.

GOING.

THE ripples break upon the beach,
   And sway the shadow of the heights;
The long slant beams that shoreward reach
   Are fretted in a thousand lights.

But on the shore the stillness dreams,
   In the blue sky the hill-tops sleep,
And through the haze of golden gleams
   The quiet shadows show more deep.

Oh silent hills! oh sleeping shore!
   Soon shall I lose you in the grey
Of stealthy evening creeping o'er,
   Of evening darkening o'er the bay.

Oh silent hills! oh sleeping shore!
   The waning light will come again,
But I shall look on you no more,
   For me morn wakens you in vain.

Sleep on, fair shore and sun-loved hills—
   I seek the land where I was born;
I seek the grey north with its chills;
   I shall not look on you at morn.

6

THE RED STAR ON THE HILL.

I WAKE before the morn, when all is still;
  No noisy crowing clamours yet to hail
That first long glimmer o'er the eastern hill.

Dim shadow rests upon the quiet vale;
  Night silence holds it yet in happy rest;
Voiceless the silver river shimmers pale;

One star peeps shily through the clouded west
  Above the moor's low blackness stretching wide
From the dusk ridges of the wood's long crest.

One light gleams redly on the mountain side
  And seems to cheer the gloom. And yet perchance
That gleam were more with thought of grief allied.

Perhaps a mother, with love-restless glance,
  Sits lonely by it, weeping in the night,
Watching the tokens of death's stern advance;

And with a trembling hand she trims the light
  That flickers strangely on his dying face,
Her son's dear face that lies so worn and white;

And prays unceasing that dear Heaven's grace
  May yet withdraw him from the Cold One's grasp,
And seeks in vain for sign of his retrace.

Perhaps this moment hears his dying gasp,
  And she, all stony in her mother-woe,
Feels a dead hand lie heavy in her clasp.

Some grief, alas! that little star's red glow
  Has surely shone on through a troubled night,
Some anguish such as pallid watchers know.

And I, who, wakened ere the morning light
  By a vague consciousness of inward pain,
Look outward through the gloom with tear-dimmed
      sight,

And, feeling power is given me in vain
  Of joying in degree surpassing speech,
Pine as one hill-born tethered to a plain,

And sigh because my days may never reach
  Fullness of life and love their need to fill—
Somewhat my thoughts my sicklier fancy teach.

6—2

Seeing that sorrow-star upon the hill,
  And reading many's sorrows by its ray,
I turn me from myself with holier will,

And know my feet tread not too rough a way,
  Though some sharp stones lie crimsoned from their
      blood;
Know I have cause to thank as well as pray.

And know moreover that, well understood,
  It is great love that gives us not all joy,
So we may learn more joy in others' good,

And learn a love more free from self's alloy,
  And so live deeply, having heavenly food,
Being love-workers in God's great employ.

A MESSENGER.

SUMMER wind surging the branches,
Dost thou come from the far away shore by the sea?
Was my love looking out on the waves astir,
Thinking "Ah would they might bear me to her,"
And did he whisper his thought to thee?
      Hast thou no message for me?

Summer wind kissing the roses,
Summer wind come to me here from the sea,
Is my true love sighing for when he was here
With his lips to the lips that he holds so dear?
Did he whisper a little word to thee?
      Hast thou no message for me?

Summer wind wooing the lily,
Summer wind come far away from the sea,
Is his love as true and as single yet
As it was when our parting tears were wet?
Did he whisper his faith and his trust to thee?
      Hast thou no message for me?

Summer wind fretting the willow,
Summer wind stolen from the shore by the sea,
Is my true love longing and lone at heart
In the bright rest-days where I have no part?
Did he not whisper his yearning to thee?
Hast thou no message for me?

Summer wind waving the ivy,
Summer wind sent to me here from the sea,
Is my true love counting the days that go by
Ere he clasp my life into his till I die?
Did he not whisper his longing to thee?
Hast thou no message for me?

THE RIVER.

THEY rode through the wood at the dead of night,
   Three knights and a lady sad and pale,
While the moon drooped down with a wan weird light,
   And a low wind sighed through the sleeping dale,
And the dead leaves rustled under their tread,
And the trees swayed muttering overhead,
And the moans of the forest pines came nigh;
   But the river rolled onward silently.

Two of the knights rode straight and strong,
   But the middle one bowed on his horse's mane,
And the winding path that they came along
   Was tracked with a terrible crimson stain,
And a terrible sound, as of dying groans,
Rose as they passed o'er the broken stones
Down where the gorge lay bare to the sky,
   And the river rolled onward silently.

And the lady wailed with a piteous woe,
   While they rode on steadily down the bank
Where the blackness of water lay below
   And the tall sedge-weeds grew lush and dank;
And the lady shrieked and prayed for grace,
But her brothers rode to the fording place
And looked with a triumphing deadly eye
   Where the river was rolling on silently.

They rode their steeds to the middle stream—
  The water stood at each horse's mouth—
They waited awhile in the dreary gleam
  While their wearied chargers slaked their drouth;
And they raised from his saddle the wounded
      knight—
One moment his armour flashed in the light,
Then an' eddy whirled and passed slowly by,
  And the river rolled onward silently.

Two plashes, a face twice seen to rise,
  The water a moment tinged with gore,
Then a gurgle heard mid the lady's cries,
  A sudden bubble and all was o'er.—
And the knights rode quickly back to the bank
Where the lady watched while her lover sank—
Three that had come and but two to hie—
  And the river rolled onward silently.

But the lady struck at her palfrey's side
  And plunged him down with a plashing bound
Into the dark stream's deepest tide,
  And they saw the white wreaths of foam whirl
      round;
And the palfrey swam to the farthest shore,
But the lady came to the land no more.
And two lay dead where but one should die.
  But the river rolled onward silently.

TWO MAIDENS.

Two maidens listening to the sea—
The younger said "The waves are glad,
The waves are singing as they break."
    The elder spake
"Sister, their murmur sounds to me
    So very sad."

Two maidens looking at a grave—
One smiled "A place of happy sleep.
It would be happy if I slept."
    The younger wept
"Oh save me from the rest you crave,
    So lone, so deep."

Two maidens gazing into life—
The younger said "It is so fair,
So warm with light and love and pride."
    The elder sighed
"It seems to me so vexed with strife,
    So cold and bare."

Two maidens face to face with death—
The elder said "With quiet bliss
Upon his breast I lay my head."
    The younger said
"His kiss has frozen all my breath,
    Must I be his?"

THE GIFT.

Oh happy glow, oh sun-bathed tree,
  Oh golden-lighted river,
A love-gift has been given me,
  And which of you is giver?

I came upon you something sad,
  Musing a mournful measure,
Now all my heart in me is glad
  With a quick sense of pleasure.

I came upon you with a heart
  Half sick of life's vexed story,
And now it grows of you a part,
  Steeped in your golden glory.

A smile into my heart has crept
  And laughs through all my being,
New joy into my life has leapt,
  A joy of only seeing!

Oh happy glow, oh sun-bathed tree,
  Oh golden-lighted river,
A love-gift has been given me,
  And which of you is giver?

IF?

IF I should die this night, (as well might be,
  So pain has on my weakness worked its will),
And they should come at morn and look on me

Lying more white than I am wont, and still
  In the strong silence of unchanging sleep,
And feel upon my brow the deepening chill,

And know me gathered to His time-long keep,
  The quiet watcher over all men's rest,
And weep as those around a death-bed weep—

There would no anguish throb my vacant breast,
  No tear-drop trickle down my stony cheek,
No smile of long farewell say " Calm is best."

I should not answer aught that they should speak,
  Nor look my meaning out of earnest eyes,
Nor press the reverent hands that mine should seek;

But, lying there in such an awful guise,
  Like some strange presence from a world unknown
Unmoved by any human sympathies,

Seem strange to them, and dreadfully alone,
   Vacant to love of theirs or agony,
Having no pulse in union with their own.

Gazing henceforth upon infinity
   With a calm consciousness devoid of change,
Watching the current of the years pass by,

And watching the long cycles onward range,
   With stronger vision of their perfect whole,
As one whom time and space from them estrange.

And they might mourn and say "The parted soul
   "Is gone out of our love; we spend in vain
"A tenderness that cannot reach its goal."

Yet I might still perchance with them remain
   In spirit, being free from laws of mould,
Still comprehending human joy and pain.

Ah me! but if I knew them as of old,
   Clasping them in vain arms, they unaware,
And mourned to find my kisses leave them cold,

And sought still some part of their life to share
   Still standing by them, hoping they might see,
And seemed to them but as the viewless air!

For so once came it in a dream to me,
   And in my heart it seemed a pang too deep,
A shadow having human life to be.

For it at least would be long perfect sleep
　Unknowing Being and all Past to lie,
Void of the growing Future, in God's keep:

But such a knowledge would be misery
　Too great to be believed.　Yet if the dead
In a diviner mood might still be nigh,

Their former life unto their death so wed
　That they could watch their loved with heavenly
　　eye,
That were a thing to joy in, not to dread.

THE HEIRESS'S WOOER.

Love! Yes, it fits thee well to talk of love!
A dainty word, a music-mellow word!
   Set it with phrases from thy bauble wit—
"A joy enthroned all other joys above;
   It is strange sweetness but to speak of it,
For one whose soul has by its thrill been stirred."

Love! What is love to beings like to thee?
An idol, glaring blank through jewelled eyes,
   Its soulless framework garnished round with gold;
A stair to mount thee to a high degree;
   A tinsel gewgaw fashioned to be sold,
Whose little value must be glozed with lies.

Thou speak of love! thou speak of love to *me!*
How have I lowered me that I should seem
   So sunk beneath myself to have thee dare
Deem I might bow my pride, my love to thee?
   If thou *couldst* love, then hadst thou known despair,
And hadst not vexed me with such useless theme.

Oh I am fair! oh very dearly fair!
I know it, I have heard the thing ere now,
   And I at lesser price can buy such praise—
Who gleams in gold finds dazzled eyes not rare—
   'Twere somewhat dear to barter youth's bright days
For the cheap flattery of a coin-paid vow.

Woo me no more. I will not hear thy prayer.
One listened once who gave thee all her heart,
   But she was poor, she could not give thee more.
Great grief no doubt! Alas thy deep despair!
   "Death anguish all thy martyred spirit tore,
"But it was duty though a death to part."

Ah! shrink: thou didst not dream I knew the tale—
She plains it now among the mouldering dead—
   Shame thee to sorrow if thou canst know shame.
How couldst thou dream thy pleadings should pre-
      vail?
   What woman-due of honour could I claim
If I could stoop with such as thou to wed?

I will not hear thee. Do not chafe me more;
It lessens me that thou hast seen one ray,
   One least faint ray of hope that thou shouldst
      snare
My fancy with thy false tongue's practised lore.
   I buy no lover, I. Waste no more care.
I pray thee seek thyself some fitter prey.

DEAD AMY.

Do I weep because she is dead?
Ah no, it is very calm in the grave,
And she needed calm, for storms were wild
And my darling was never very brave:
Now she smiles in sleep like a little child
    Dreaming at night in its happy bed:
    Why should I weep for her dead?

She was very young and bright,
But she could not laugh her sorrows away
As I, who am stronger and harder, could do,
Though the brown of my locks grew dimmed with
       grey:
But she, her heart was too simple and true
    To jest with grief, and her cheek grew white—
    It was once so fair and bright.

Perhaps it was all for the best
For both, though it leaves me so very lone,
I could hardly have borne so much distress,
If it had not been all and only my own.
Ah well! her smile was a thing to bless
    My sharpest pain, but nought pains her rest,
    So I think it is all for the best.

For I think I must have gone mad
Had I seen her grow worn and early old
With the care and the burden of toilsome days.
To see her pallid with hunger and cold
And pained by want in a thousand ways,
  To see her sweet face grow rigid and sad,
  Surely I must have gone mad !

But she would have borne it all
And still have smiled, but she could not bear
All the shame and the loathing that others draw
On our name, and our burden of lonely care—
For we had not many friends that were true,
  So had small love-comfortings in our fall,
  And she could not bear it at all.

She did not often weep
But grew more silent and still every day,
And seldom moved, but sat white and sad ;
So when I saw she must pass away
I had almost the courage to be glad—
  Ah well ! my darling has happy sleep,
  And so I do not weep.

A MARCH NIGHT.

WHITE moonbeams, trembling through the night
  Upon the wind-stirred lawn, and swayed
By sudden gusts in tossing light
  On bare March boughs along the glade,

Shine clear upon the surge-lashed head,
  Shine clear upon the rock-set bay :
The sea has had enough of dead,
  And the brave ships plunge on their way.

Wild river, flying from the wind
  On, past the quiet village homes
With their long furrowed fields behind,
  To leap into the mad sea-foams,

Wail echoing to the cruel sea,
  Wail for us that it spare its prey :
Mothers are weeping on bent knee,
  And the frail ships toss on their way.

Fierce whirlwinds, warring on our plain
  With the strong trees that heave and crash,
Hurling away the pelts of rain,
  Shrill shrieking through the rattling sash,

Faint, weary from thy rage, and die :
  Far off the billows writhe in spray,
We waken at thy voice and sigh,
  And the dear ships plunge on their way.

THE HIDDEN WOUND.

THE lady spoke with a merry scorn,
  Laughed with scorn when they talked of care,
"Oh you talk and talk, but the tale is worn
  Of poisoned love that kills by despair,
There *may* be love, but for lover's sake
Never was heart yet known to break."
And she turned away with a haughty smile—
But a deep wound bled in her heart the while.

And "Life is too full of change," she said,
  "That grief, like joy, should not pass away.
And why for a dreaming moment fled
  Should one sorrow the livelong day?
And what though a fickle love be lost,
Is it worth the light of a life for cost?
But *I* would laugh with such love to part"—
And all the while blood oozed from her heart.

She decked her beauty in silk and lace,
  She set rich gems in her braided hair,
And shone in a glory of youth and grace;
  Men's hearts leaped high that she was so fair;
Her proud eye flashed with a queenly glance,
Her step was light and fleet in the dance,
Her laugh rang out with a silver sound—
But the red drops ran from the hidden wound.

7—2

There fell on her face no sorrow-sign,
  Nothing the slow sharp pain to speak,
Save beneath her eye one soft dark line,
  One soft white edge to each rich rosed cheek;
Her large dark eyes grew strangely bright,
And who has seen tear-drops dull their light?
And she spoke glad words with a wondrous smile—
But the life-blood oozed from her heart the while.

Weeping they laid her low in the grave,
  She had not wept to pass away,
And "Surely" they said "she was very brave;
  With a life as bright as the summer-day,
To look on death with a tearless eye
Almost as though she wished to die!"
And they never knew of their early dead
How the deep deep wound in her heart had bled.

But one in strife with an awful dread
  Asked himself "Did I slay her indeed?
She was so young—and now she is dead.
  Yet can one small wound so deadly bleed?"
But some one came and stood by his side,
A sweet fair face—and he loved his bride—
And he thought "Ah! no, for life is too fair
"That one should sink under any despair;
"In truth not long could such wound have bled"—
  But she who had loved him so was dead.

SAFE.

WILD wintry wind, storm through the night,
   Dash the black clouds against the sky,
Hiss through the billows seething white,
   Fling the rock-surf in spray on high. ·

Hurl the high seas on harbour bars,
   Madden them with thy havock-shriek
Against the crimson beacon-stars—
   Thy rage no more can make me weak.

The ship rides safely in the bay,
   The ship that held my hope in her—
Whirl on, wild wind, in thy wild fray,
   We hear our whispers through the stir.

PASSING AWAY.

PASSING away from you, love,
And you look so sad, sitting there by my bed,
And I know you are thinking "How will it be?
"She is the meaning of living to me,
    "How can I live with her dead?"

Passing away from you, love,
Growing weaker and weaker every day:
Soon you will sit near me, ah! so alone,
For I shall not turn to you, I your own,
    I shall not heed what you say.

Passing away from you, love,
It will not be long now before the last:
We are thinking about it, feign as we will,
While I seem to sleep and you are so still,
    Our clasped hands holding fast.

One same thought in our minds,
How strangely lone you will feel in your home
When I have gone out of your waking days
And you dream of our life in a sorrowful maze
    When the desolate evenings come.

But, love, it cannot be lost,
The life that is ours, that I leave to you yours,
As something far more than a memory;
We know it something too real to die,
    It is love, and love endures.

    It will follow you into the new;
You cannot part it from you, chance what will,
You could not live as if I had not been;
So to you long hence when my grave is green,
    Love, I must be somewhat still.

    Passing away from you, love,
And the weakness and weariness grow into pain,
So that the last would seem dropping asleep
If it were not for you. But one rests in God's
    keep,
    So I think you will find me again.

TOO FAITHFUL.

Too fond and faithful, wilt thou vainly yet
   Waste love on one who does not ask it now
And, having wronged thee, seeks but to forget?

A fairer face smiles on his love, and thou,
   Thou with thy truth and fervour, stand aside,
Thou nobler-natured to her beauty bow.

There lingers in thee yet this much of pride
   Thàt he who thus has wronged himself and thee
Could never win thy truth whate'er betide,

Since in thine eyes he never more may be
   So true and great that thou couldst bend to him,
Oh never more! Why is thy heart not free?

Oh wilt thou weep because his eyes are dim?
   And wilt thou blush because his choice is shame
Falling on one whose love is but a whim?

An idle whim to stir a languid heart,
   A business chaffering of the more and less
And rise and falling of the marriage mart.

Yet is it cause to deepen thy distress
   That he shall suffer for his misplaced trust?
For did he come into thy life to bless?

He buys a bauble something touched with rust,
   Passing through many hands that did not hold,
Its lustre deadened by the market's dust.

But what to thee, if he for this has sold
   His faith, his living heart, his nobler mind,
And given gold for that which is not gold?

Oh better that he should rest ever blind,
   Better for him—but should he wake to see
The gem, he dreamed so pure, of paltriest kind,

Too fond and faithful, what were that to thee?
   Thou hast thy sorrow; wherefore look beyond
To sorrow for his sorrow that shall be?

Too fond and faithful, weak in being fond,
   False to thyself by faithfulness to him,
Since he has freed thee wherefore art thou bond?

And if his cup hold poison to the rim,
   Dregged with life's malady beyond life's cure,
Why should its bitter drops to thine o'erbrim?

And yet, if thou hast love so deep and pure
   That, whatsoever change the years shall bring,
Before the sight of God it may endure,

And if it seem to thee a holy thing
  That, should he need it in his day of pain,
Thou mayst have sister power of comforting,

Well, if thy love be thus, let it remain;
  Thou wilt not fear to name it in thy prayer,
As though it were some passion wild and vain.

Well, let it be, it may make less that care
  Centred in self thou canst not wholly quell,
If others' not thine own its place shall share.

SHADOW.

Dark, dark, as when dull autumn yields his breath ;
  Strange days when will ye change and let me see
A little sunshine ere I pass in death?

Oh ! sadder than long sad hours of the night
  When watching closing eyes that will not wake
Ever again to hold the morning light.

Oh long long heavy hours and how long still?
  Strangest of all is it that ye who have
Such deadening power should not have power to
    kill.

Oh ! days all night—but, if the morning come,
  I shall awaken, in whichever world,
With opening eyes, and know myself at home.

SUNLIGHT.

BLITHE birds, sing to the spring;
The spring has waked on this young April day,
With all your tiny voice give welcoming,
The spring has waked, we waken and are gay.

So long the winter lowered,
So weary long upon the mourning earth;
So tremblingly the shivering March blooms flowered
And waned, touched with the frost death from their
       birth.

So long the skies were low
And always darkening downwards cold and grey,
So long forgotten was the sunlight glow,
So far far in the past the last bright day.

And now the spring has come;
Sing, sing, wild twittering birds, sing from the trees,
You who, as I, can only feel a home
In the great earth when glad with days like these.

We waken, you and I, from winter chills,
With the new sunny days, with the young flowers;
Sing with me, sing your clearest happiest trills,
The riches of the springtime all are ours.

A MOTHER'S CRY.

CHILD, child, will you have me die?
You are merciless in your mute despair.
Will there never be love again
Between us two?—Oh! life of my life,
Have I only lived for my mother care,
And now are we lost in a silent strife?
Child, is not yours also your mother's pain?
   And you look on me stonily!

   What was there left me to do?
Could I give my child to a libertine,
Could I give to one mocking God?
I would die to make him that which he aped,
But could I dare—Oh! child, were you mine
But that I should trample the bliss you shaped?
But the lonely cold home beneath the sod
   Than his had been better for you.

Ah! surely if you had learned
By bitter taste the ill that I dread
You would think "Did my mother sleep,
Or did her love, that she yielded her child
To one whom it was but a curse to wed?
Yes she has held my happiness cheap,
For *I* by my young heart's love was beguiled,
       But *she* must have surely discerned."

       And now, do you think my cry
Went not wildly up in the sleepless night
With an anguish and storm of prayer
That God would spare me this bitterness?
Do you think I did not struggle with might
While the blood in my veins seemed less and less,
Sickened with pain before I could dare
       To fashion him that reply?

       Because you believed in him yet,
Because you loved him, and I—my own,
Think you I do not turn to you
With a yearning passionate agony?
And must I go mourning and alone
A love-reft mother? Ah! if you knew
How I steal in the night to where you lie
       And I watch—ah! my cheeks so wet!

But you turn your heart from me,
You sit with a pale and sorrowful face,
Hushed and listless the live-long day
Till I even wish I could see you weep,
For you never stir from the selfsame place,
Your hands in your lap, and no word you say,
And I scarce know whether you wake or sleep,
  Though I creep to your side to see.

  Alas! and I hear your heart
Speak through the stillness its bitter plaint
"I who have loved my mother so dear,
I bleed from a deadly wound within,
And she it is"—Oh! my heart grows faint.
Child, *my* child, have you not one tear,
Not one smile for your mother to win?
  Do not *I* also bear my part?

  Yes I who must see you pine,
Worn with the weight of your heavy cross,
Paler and thinner day by day,
And know that *my* lips pronounced your doom,
Thus for my gain and your love for loss!—
Oh hear, my God, how I cry from the gloom,
Shall not this darkness vanish away?—
  Oh my child art thou no more mine!

DREAMING.

THE quivering ripples all dancing now,
   Tossing each other the glow,
A hundred lights on the lowest bough
   Flickering to and fro,
A humming murmur of tree and stream,
   And the voices of wild birds glad,
And I lie lost in a languid dream,
   Too happy not to be sad.

A happy dream of a sweet spring hour
   In the arch of an avenue
Where the chestnuts are dropping a snowy shower
   And the sunbeam lies on the dew,
And a voice is answering very low,
   In mine a timid hand lies,
And a tangle of golden hair aglow
   Droops shadows on downcast eyes.

And I should be conning a learned book,
   (Study makes a man grow wise),
But I lie tranced by the spell of the brook,
   Lulled into sweet reveries,
Lost in a dream of a leafy aisle
   And two lovers whispering there,
Lost in a dream of a sunny smile
   And the glitter of golden hair.

A WEDDING.

A BRIDEGROOM waits in the green churchyard—
Waits and waits, but he speaks no word,
The smile on his lips is cold and hard,
His rigid look turns never aside,
The folds of his cloak are never stirred.
A bridegroom waits for his young young bride
By a grave in the still churchyard.

A maiden comes to her wedding plight—
Roses burn on her white soft cheeks,
The gleam of her eyes is clear and bright,
She looks before with a gaze that reads
In her bridegroom's calm the peace she seeks.
A maiden comes for the rest she needs,
And joys in her wedding plight.

She lays her head on his quiet breast—
"My bridegroom is holy and wise,
Lap me, sweet death, in thy solemn rest,"
And looks with a love-look fond and brave,
And thrills in his clasp with happy eyes.
The bridegroom clasps in the silent grave
His young young bride to his breast.

8

THE SETTING STAR.

SET pallid star, the yellow light
  Is waking o'er the slopes of corn,
The autumned woods upon the height
  Are golden-pencilled by the morn.

Set fading star, the happy sky
  Is blushing at the kiss of day,
Set ere thy saddened lustre die
  In the rich rays that track his way.

Set darkened star, the silver stream
  That loved thy image through the night
Will lose it soon in fuller gleam,
  Set ere it learn a new delight.

Tremble no longer on the brink,
  Droop downward, seeking skies of rest,
Droop downward, setting star, and sink
  Before the twilight leaves the west.

TO ONE OF MANY.

WHAT! wilt thou throw thy stone of malice now,
Thou dare to scoff at him with scorn or blame?
He is a thousand times more great than thou:
Thou, with thy narrower mind and lower aim,
Wilt thou chide him and not be checked by shame?

He hath done evil—God forbid my sight
Should falter where I gaze with loving eye,
That I should fail to know the wrong from right.
He hath done evil—let not any tie
Of birth or love draw moral sense awry.

And though my trust in him is yet full strong.
I may not hold him guiltless, in the dream
That wrong forgiven is no longer wrong,
And, looking on his error, fondly deem
That he in that he erreth doth but *seem*.

8—2

I do not soothe me with a vain belief;
He hath done evil, therefore is my thought
Of him made sadness with no common grief.
But thou, what good or truth has in . thee wrought
That thou shouldst hold thee more than him in aught?

He will redeem his nature, he is great
In inward purpose past thy power to scan,
And he will bear his meed of evil fate
And lift him from his fall a nobler man,
Hating his error as a great one can.

And what art thou to look on him and say
"Ah! he has fallen whom they praised, but know
My foot is sure"? Upon thy level way
Are there the perils of the hills of snow?
Yea, he has fallen, but wherefore art thou low?

Speak no light word of him, for he is more
Than thou canst know—and ever more to me,
Though he has lessened the first faith I bore,
Than thou in thy best deeds couldst ever be;
Yea, though he fall again, not low like thee.

LOOKING DOWNWARDS.

THE sunlights waver from rock to rock,
   And the pied clouds come and go,
And the restless bay, with a flickering mock,
   Quivers back shadow and glow.
Change and change, as all changes in life,
But through all I hear the same voice of strife,
Surges of seas and their sullen shock
   At the base of the crag below.

Surges far down below at the base,
   How many feet, can I guess,
From me in my high cliff resting-place,
   Alone with my weariness?
How many feet?—And out and away
The surges roll back to the tossing bay;
And if I lay whelmed in their seething race
   Would the world laugh any the less?

A moment or two and a troubled heart
   Might be still in a troubled sea—
And surely, if that were all, one's part
   Might be played out and sleep might be;

For the dead are quiet and never weep.
But sorrow of life is nobler than sleep
And a heart may be strong though it writhe
    smart.
  Oh! heart be thou strong in me.

Change and change! and the sunlights shake
  And flit at the wind's wild hest,
And the clouds and shadows gather and break,
  Change and not any rest!
And never a light of man's life so still
But its good may be darked with some wind-waft
Yet surely to sleep is less than to wake,
  And sorrow of life is best.

ON THE LAKE.

A SUMMER mist on the mountain heights,
  A golden haze in the sky,
A glow on the shore of sleeping lights,
  And shadows lie heavily.

Far in the valley the town lies still,
  Dreaming asleep in the glare,
Dreamily near purs the drowsy rill,
  Dreams are afloat in the air.

Dreaming above us the languid sky,
  Dreaming the slumbering lake,
And we who rest floating listlessly
  Say, love, do we dream or wake?

TO AND FRO.

THERE is much shadow on this sunlit earth,
  And sorrow lingers deep in laughing eyes,
Sad echoes tremble mid glad peals of mirth,
  Low wailings whisper through rich melodies.

You cannot say of any one you know,
  "I see his life, I know him very blest."
For would he tell you of the canker woe
  That preys upon his being unconfessed?

You cannot think in any festive place
  Of mirth and pastime and smiles flashed on all
There is no mimic weary of his face,
  No actor longing for the curtain's fall.

Among the dancers cruel spectres float
  And chill their victims with a dull distress,
And, sighing through the measure's clearest note,
  Weird voices murmur, full of bitterness.

Old sorrows fester on in aching hearts,
  New sorrows rack them with hot spasm pain;
Who knows? The ball-room actors play their parts,
  And we smile with them and discern no strain.

If one should say "This is a doubtful word,
　That men so sorrowing can cheat our sense"
Yet let him own when grief his soul has stirred
　He has been merry with gay eloquence.

And that is best.　For what would it avail
　If he should say "Lo, I am very sad"
To idle hearers, though they heard his tale
　And ceased a little moment to be glad?

But each heart keeps its sorrow for its own
　Nor bares its wound to the chill general gaze;
Men laugh together... if they weep alone:
　But sorrow walks in all the wide world's ways.

What, will you fly? her step is very fleet,
　Her freezing touch will seize you unawares.
Look on her, never grovel at her feet,
　For he is hers for ever who despairs.

Wait calmly; as she waits on that old plain,
　The stony smiler on the desert sand,
Smiling upon old pride's long-cycled wane,
　Smiling unchanged upon a saddened land.

She saw the glories of the ancient days,
　She ever sees the tombs of buried kings,
She has not lost the quiet of her gaze
　Looking a silence deep with solemn things.

The great sand-surges press upon her close,
  She in eternal calm looks out above—
And who shall look upon a waste of woes
  With such grand patience which no change may
    move?

Yet wait; let the great desert clouds whirl by,
  And sunlight once more floods upon the plain.
Yet wait; the foolish leaf that flies the blast
  Grows never greenly on the bough again.

Yet wait; for sorrow's self is not all sad:
  Put forth your hand and draw her veil aside;
Behold, what secret of masked smiles she had,
  What royal lovegifts in one cloked hand hide.

You will not say those were your saddest years,
  In which you sorrowed. Void is worse than pain.
And many a rich bloom grows because of tears;
  And we see Heaven's lights more when our lights
    wane.

Ah! who knows what is ill from what is well?
  And we, who see no more than we are shown
Of others' hearts, can we so much as tell
  If grief or joy be chiefest in our own?

For sunlight gleams upon this shadowed earth,
  Sunlight and shadow waver to and fro,
And sadness echoes in the voice of mirth,
  And music murmurs through the wail of woe.

AFTERWARDS.

A LITTLE word not said,
A little word begged in vain—
And oh! I would be rather lying dead,
If only then he would love me again.

A foolish touch of pride,
Pride more than half meant to please—
And I, that should deck me a May-morn bride,
Sit weeping alone by the bare March trees.

And soon, soon, May will come,
And soon, soon, May will be gone,
But my love will have made him a lonely home,
And I must be loving him, loving alone.

How strange he could not tell
His peace was made at a word;
If I acted my anger never so well,
Could he catch no echoes from love-words once
    heard?

Too late for him to know!
Too late! Let him think me cold,
And loveless and false as he says; better so.
But my love, my love, I love more than of old.

Oh, best love of my heart,
Oh love, my lover no more,
You have ruled it firmly that we should part,
But you cannot make me less yours than before.

Yours, yours, yours alone,
Still yours though you will not care,
Yours with a love that has been but half shown,
For 'tis fit to be coy...and I did not dare.

You'll not know all your life
What loving you means to me.
I thought "Oh the bold brave love of his wife!"
But, oh! once my betrothed, who shall she now be?

OUR LILY.

THE angels dropped us a wee white flower,
   Yes surely it was from heaven it fell:
Then came the wind and the beating shower,
   But it was sheltered down in our dell.

And it grew and grew through the fresh spring days,
   The sweetest blossom that ever God made:
Then came the sun with his scorching rays,
   But down in our dell there was cool and shade.

And it grew and grew in the summer air,
   It was a lily of Paradise,
And we watched it open each day more fair,
   Nothing on earth so dear in our eyes.

And tenderly we fenced it about,
   And the angels of Heaven they guarded it well:
Then came the time of the sultry drought,
   But the brook ran clear in our shadowy dell.

So it grew and grew, come foul, come fair,
   And never a soil on its whiteness stood,
And, because the angels made it their care,
   From good and bad it drew only good.

And oh! the blessing to see it grow,
  And I think that our hearts both grew as it grew,
And oh! we loved it, we loved it so!
  And we called it ours and thought we spoke true.

But at last it had grown so sweet and so white,
  That the angels could not leave it us still,
And they came and took it away in the night,
  One sad still night when the mist was chill.

And oh! the blank when our lily went!
  And we look in each other's faces alone,
And we say sometimes "Well it was but lent,"
  Yet, even in Heaven, we call it our own.

And I think it must be meant for us at last,
  For would God have made us love it in vain?
Perhaps, if the gates of Heaven were past,
  His hand would give us our blossom again.

ON THE SHORE.

THE angry sunset fades from out the west,
  A glimmering greyness creeps along the sea,
Wild waves be hushed and moan into your rest,
  Soon will all earth be sleeping, why not ye?

Far off the heavens deaden o'er with sleep,
  The purple twilight darkens on the hill,
Why will ye only ever wake and weep?
  I weary of your sighing, oh! be still.

But ever ever moan ye by the shore,
  While all your trouble surges in my breast.
Oh waves of trouble surge in me no more,
  Or be but still awhile and let me rest.

GLAD WAVES.

Leap on, glad waves, in summer glee,
  A voice of joy has come to-day,
A voice of joy has come to me—
  Leap on glad waves, flash through the bay.

Laugh, merry waves, laugh back the light,
  Laugh back the light that is not yours,
On me another's joy suns bright—
  Dash, laughing waves, against your shores.

Surge on, bright waves, beneath bright skies,
  Voice out delight; but through your speech
There ever swells a voice of sighs—
  Break, sighing waves, against the beach.

Sigh on, bright waves, through summer glee:
  While on my thoughts a joy floats bright,
A bitterness is deep in me—
  Sad waves laugh back the happy light.

DESERTED.

No, mother, I am not sad :
Why think me sad? I was always still,
You remember, even when my heart was most glad
And you used to let me dream at my will;
And now I like better to watch the sea
And the calm sad sky than to laugh with the rest,
You know they are full of chatter and glee,
    And I like the quietness best.

Nay, mother, you look so grave.
I know what you're thinking and will not say;
But you need not fear; I am growing brave
Now that the pain is passing away,
And I never weep for him now when alone,
For perhaps it was better—who can tell?—
That it ended so. I shall soon be well
    Now that the hardest is known.

I am so much stronger to-day
I can look at all past and think how it grew
And how by degrees it faded away,
That light of my life. Ah ! when I first knew

I had only been a plaything to him
Through all my loving, it seemed so strange.
If the high noontide at once grew night-dim
   It would not be such a change.

   I wonder I did not die.
Mother, I'll own it you now I am strong,
I used to wake in the night and lie
Wishing and wishing it might not be long-
Oh! it was wicked, and you all so kind,
How could I wish to bring you a grief?
But too much unhappiness makes one blind
   To all but one's own relief.

   I am not so wicked now;
You need not fear I am hoping that still,
I am learning to lean on God, and I bow,
Yes I think I bow my heart to His will.
I found it a long hard struggle to make,
To clasp my sorrow and say " It is best,"
But, believe it, you need not fear for my sake;
   Yes, mother, I am at rest:

   Yet, listen, if I should die soon—
And I know what they say, though you hide it from
      me—
Mother, you'll grant me my last-asked boon,
That you'll try not to think it his fault, and if he,

Mother, if he should seek you some day,
You will not make him a hard reply,
But tell him, before I passed away,
 I sent him kind good-bye.

Mother, kiss me, do not cry.
I could not keep from speaking of this;
It is nothing to say "If I should die,"
It cannot bring death more near than it is;
And I am much stronger. You shall not weep—
Who is it tells me that weeping is wrong?
But let me lean on your lap and sleep,
 I lay waking last night too long.

PERJURED.

In my dream he came—
I lonely in a slumbrous twilight mind,
Seeing the water ripple to the wind
And the leaf-shadows quiver on my dress,
Hearing the answer of the sycamore
And the corn surge like waves on a sand shore,
I lulled into a pensive tenderness,
Gathering all life into a heart of love—
　　And then he came—
Or some sound rose as if he spoke my name.
Was it the wind in the sycamore above?

　　But I saw him—*him*,
Not looking with the face of one long dead;
But the last sunbeams playing on his head,
Flashing its chestnut gold, and in his eyes
The light that came because he looked on me.
Oh love, but I *did* love thee, though there be
A past of wrong between us, though new ties
Have barred between me even and thy grave.
　　Yes, my eyes were dim,
My heart weak at that sudden thought of him,
And so I saw him there—oh heart be brave.

What now is regret?
Or what can I atone towards him now
When penitence is sin? for the wife's vow
Leaves room for no dead lover; and—if they
Who die away from us can love us still—
He could not love me though he pass the ill
My falseness worked him in a shameful day
And sad—Ah sadder than for him for me.
    Hush, then no regret,
My folly and my fault far off is set.
Oh worst remorse which never may be free!

HOW THE BROOK SINGS.

THE long low sunbeams eastward fall,
  Long yellow glories lie
Between the trees, on the ivied wall,
  On the brooklet singing by.

The brook is singing low to me—
  You cannot hear what it says—
Its voice is rich and glad with the glee,
  With the love of happy days.

Ah! the shadows have dimmed its glow!
  Yet still it sings to me
Of joy and love that were long ago,
  And joy and love that shall be.

THE LAKE.

I.

SHE said no word, but looked on him,
  And then he knew that she was won;
And all the world grew far and dim,
  And they were two beneath the sun.
And "Oh my love" and "Oh my own"
  And "Leave the little hand in mine :"
While from below the lake's long moan
  Came upwards from the shore's low line

"Oh! love, through all a stormy life
  That brought not rest nor any bliss,
While angry in the hard world's strife,
  I looked for such an hour as this."
"Oh! love, through all a cold hushed youth,
  I never dreamed such ·joy in store."
And so they plighted lovers' truth :
  And the grey lake moaned on the shore.

II.

She stood upon the silent hill
  And watched the creeping shadows grow:
And "Surely he must love me still:"
  And "I would give the world to know."
And "It was here we said we loved:"
  And "Love, through all I love thee more."
While slow the creeping shadows moved,
  And the dim lake sighed on the shore.

And slow and singly over head
  The white stars looked on her alone:
And "Oh! my love, they make me wed,
  And not one word to claim thine own!"
And "Not one word, love, not one word!"
  And "Oh my love if thou wert dead!"
While through the pines the night-winds stirred,
  And the dark lake moaned in its bed.

III.

He watched the sunlights on the lake,
  The shadow of a yellow cloud:
And "It was here my love I spake,
  And it was here our love we vowed."

And "Women love the man that's near,
  And more than love count wealth and show:"
While from the sky a lark sang clear,
  And the blue lake plashed light below.

And "So soon dead! And yet I would
  It had been sooner; for she seemed
So good—What then? he calls her good,
  Her husband, dreams her what I dreamed."
And "Oh dead love!" And "Oh lost love!
  Dead with a baby on thy breast!"
And the glad lark trilled on above,
  And the lulled lake basked into rest.

IN THE SUNSHINE.

CAROL it merrily out, blithe birds,
Trill from the branches, chirp from the eaves,
Whisper it cheerily, waving leaves,
Chirrup it, grasshopper, shrill to green earth,
Chime, all day's voices, in love and mirth—
    My joy is too full for words.

Laugh it in sparkles, quivering brook,
Plash it, clear fall, in your trebling showers,
Breathe it in perfume, fresh-scented flowers,
Smile, smile, all my gladness, tender sky,
Speak, all day's glories—I cannot, I,
    She must learn it all in a look.

Murmur it softly, far-off tide,
Surge it lovingly, billowing corn—
I who have sighed for the day I was born,
Have no joy words for the thoughts that rise—
Well she must read them all in my eyes,
    She will look in them now, my bride!

NIGHT WHISPERS.

THERE crept a whisper through the night
"All is dying, all is dead:
Turn away thy wearied sight,
Rest thee in thine earthy bed:
Life is sorrow, life is pain,
And thy prayer for strength is vain,
Yield thee to thyself and weep,
Weep thy weakness into sleep,
Death has slumber sweet and deep."

There crept a whisper through the night
"All is dying, all is dead;
All the glory and delight,
All the beauty, all have fled,
And thy youth is lorn of life:
Wilt thou wage with Sorrow strife?
Ah! the vainness! canst thou raise
From the dust thy drooping days
That faint beneath her deadly gaze?"

There crept a whisper through the night
"All is dying, all is dead :
Hateful is the morning's light,
Hateful is the evening's red :
All is hateful, all is pain,
Rest comes never more again.
Hope and love for aye are o'er,
Peace and joy return no more,
Follow them to Death's still shore."

But I answered to the Night
"All is dying, all is dead,
All the glory and delight
All the beauty, all have fled :
I am heavy and oppressed,
And I know Death has calm rest,
And I know Life has much care,
But I will not mar my prayer
With the cries of weak despair."

So I answered to the Night
"All is dying, all is dead,
But I have not dimmed all sight
With the bitter tears I shed.
And I know Life's darkest ways
Are crossed by golden heaven-rays,
Well I feel Death's rest were sweet,
But I know it is more meet
To seek high goal with onward feet."

Crept the whisper through the night
"All is dying, all is dead."
But I answered "This is right,
Not to shrink with coward dread
From a pain that must be borne.
I know Life's good and have not lost
All trust though trust has dearly cost,
Nor faith in Heaven though tempest tossed."

And the whisper still crept by
"All is dying, all is dead,"
But I said "Though all should die
Nothing is quite perished."

THE BLUSH-ROSE.

FREE forest bird, beat the wild wing,
  Fly north and south the whole day through,
To north, to south, fly wavering,
  On every side the skies are blue.

Fly north and south through all the day,
  Fly westward when the skies are red,
Perch thee upon the topmost spray
  Of the blush-rose in its mossy bed.

Sing to my love thy tenderest song,
  (Each evening she bends o'er the tree
I set and she has watched so long),
  And see, sweet bird, thou sing of me.

But roses die, and memory
  May call to sleeping love in vain;
What if the rose should bloom and die
  Before I seek my love again?

And would my love for ever sigh,
  Or would she learn a lighter strain?
What if the tree's last bloom should die
  And I not seek my love again?

A BRIDE.

WEEP for me, Weep for me;
I am young to die.
But they say "Who talks of death?
Maiden, weave thy wedding wreath."
Weep for me, Weep for me
With my wedding nigh.

Weep for me, Weep for me—
Jewels on my breast,
Velvet robes all seamed with gold,
An Earl's young son my train to hold.
Weep for me, Weep for me
At the wedding feast.

Weep for me, Weep for me—
All at my command,
Serfs and knights and lands and halls
All his bride's my bridegroom calls.
Weep for me, Weep for me
When he takes my hand.

Weep for me, Weep for me—
Ere the spring goes by
My murdered love will make me his:
He swears it me with each night's kiss.
Weep for me, Weep for me;
I am young to die.

MARY LOST.

Dance, dance on thy way, thou rippling stream,
   Laugh to the summer skies—
But joy lies dead in thy laughing gleam,
   Like Love in a false love's eyes.

Chant, plashing river, thy even lay,
   Gush liquid harmonies—
But the mirth of thy music has passed away,
   And its burden is turned to sighs.

Flash in clear shallows and rock-rimmed deeps,
   Glitter in sun-bright pride—
But the gloom of that cypress where Mary sleeps
   Casts shadows on all thy tide.

Storm thy way at the foot of the hill,
   Dash o'er the bars of stone—
But the stream of my life is checked and still,
   And the force of its flow is gone.

THE LAND OF HAPPY DREAMS.

In the land of happy dreams
Through a short dream-life I dwelt—
Was it very long ago?
There was music in the streams,
Vague weird voices soft and low!
Purple mists would rise and melt,
Golden vapours floated by,
Trancing all with mystery,
With a sweet strange mystery
In the land of happy dreams.

Ah the land of happy dreams!
Ah the beauty! Ah the love!
Was it very long ago?
Can I tell? Long, long it seems
Since a wild wild wave of woe—
Ah I strove! ah vainly strove!—
Bore me from the golden shore.
I shall dream there nevermore;
I shall rest me nevermore
In the land of happy dreams.

THE SHADOW OF A CLOUD.

ONLY a moment ago, and the beams
    Were dancing along the ivied wall,
And the leaves were aglow to the happy gleams:
    But the cloud has darkened it all.

Only a moment ago, and the brook
    Shook in a golden smile down the fall
Bright to its heart by the sky's kind look:
    But the cloud has darkened it all.

A moment ago—does it need no more,
    And the heart is dulled by a thing so small?
Was it I who was glad to the very core?
    But the cloud has darkened it all.

FAIRIES' CHATTER.

OH ! come, the hour to us belongs :
    Slumber seals tired sleepers' eyes,
    Hushed are the glad melodies,
    The voice of laughter and of songs,
    The echoes of the joy-winged feet
    Beating time in cadence fleet
    To the minstrel measures sweet :
Hushed the merry greybeard's jest,
And the fair child's glee in its tricksome freak,
      And the low love-word
That brought the quick flush to the maiden's cheek,
That brought the strange thrill to the maiden's breast,
And echoes in dreams through her happy rest
While she smiles asleep through the night's last hours,
Though she played with her knots of mimic flowers
      As though 'twere unheard :
Hushed the buzz of friendly talk :
Hushed upon the frost-crisped walk
The footfall of the home-bound guest :

And there wakes no sound
Of human life through the ancient house
Save the long-drawn breath of sleep.
But the gossiping crickets chirp their round,
Merry, so merry, chirp chirp, cheep cheep,
And the stealthy mouse
Scuds with small pattering feet through the house
While her kinsfolk shrill from the panelled wall.
And the log, yet ablaze,
Crackles and crisps in the chimney deep,
And the last flame rays
Gurgle and bubble and flicker and leap
And spurt into fire ere they fade out quite,
Spurt and flash ere they die.
Oh! come, ere they die,
To laugh in the light of the crimson glow,
And chase on the floor, as they come and go,
The frolicsome bars of light,
With feet that fly
As blithe and as noiseless to and fro.
Ah! the flames are dead,
And the smouldering log burns a dim dull red;
And there is no light in the ancient hall,
But from the great moon shining white.
We cannot see her but she is there,
Outside in the night;
For look where the shimmering halos fall
On the frosted panes till they glitter fair

Like fretted silver brilliant set,
And calm St Lucy, carved in stone
And corbelled 'neath the oriel's roof,
Is crowned with moonbeam coronet:
And back the deadened rays are thrown
From the old knightly coats of proof,
And the battered shields and spears
Ranged there uselessly for years:
And the wreathed hollies, every one,
Sparkle as though newly wet
In April's rain against the sun.

There is little change in the ancient hall
Since days too far for these men's ken,
And *we* have not changed, but the lives of men
And their ways and their words are altered all.
And how is Sir Hugh, by his Christmas fire,
Portly and ruddy, in sober prate,
As he sips his wine with complacent smile,
Of rights and wrongs and needs of the state,
(The children playing him tricks the while),
Like old Sir Hugo his far off sire,
 Hugo, whose sword was ever red in fray
 With the blood of many foemen slain,
 Holding the lordly feast in knight's array
  Amid his vassal train?
Ah! they are gone, the noble knights
Whose pennons waved in gallant fights;

They are gone, the loving eyes
Lighting them to high emprize.
Ah! their day has passed away,
 Their day that was *our* day,
When all about the English land
 Blithely dwelt the fairy band,
 Something feared and yet well-loved,
 When through homes of men we moved,
 Holding viewless fellowship
 With the toilers true of heart,
 Bearing in their labours part,
 Giving gifts and sweet content;
 But to men of evil bent
 Dealing crooked punishment,
 Cross and loss and ache and nip;
 Thwarting the unwilling toil
 Of the sluggard leaden-eyed,
 Lowering with shame-edged despite
  The heart of pride;
 Snatching from the miser's grip,
 While he told it in the night,
 The red gold stained with hidden soil
  Of fraud and shame.
So we blessed the good, and we checked the ill—
But now the days of our power are gone,
We love the land and we linger still,
But sundered from mortals now, and none
  Joy or fear at our name.

None love us now, none as they loved,
    The whilome dwellers in this hall,
They whom we honoured and well proved,
    Loved by the fairies passing all,
        They who would vaunt to trace
        Back to a far-off day
        Their lineage from a fairy race,
And tell how Amys gained for bride
        The gold-haired valley fay,
Wherefore this valley shall abide
        With their true heirs for aye.
They knew the fairies ever watched their way,
    They gloried in such lot;
For them we love their children of to-day
    Who know us not,
And think us wholly faded from the earth,
    Shades that have ceased to be.
And yet for our remembrance have they spared
        The twisted tree,
    All ringed and lichened with its years,
That saw beneath the moon our dancing mirth,
        So bears our name till now,
Have propped the branches time has bent and bared,
    Have let the waving grassknots grow
    Unvexed by formal gardener's shears,
And the long sprays unlopped droop o'er
From the lush bramble hedge grown round.

This for love of the dear fays
"Who," say they, "in ancient days
Made here by night their meeting ground;
Fays departed from old haunts for evermore,
    Gone with the times of yore."

And therefore do we tend them yet,
    Though we be left unthanked, unknown.
Now, ere the full-faced moon be set,
    Now, while the still hours are our own,
        Light will we glide
        To the sleeper's side,
    And bring sweet dreams of that which shall betide,
    And bring sweet dreams of that which has
            gone by
        In a happy past;
    And, in a vague dream-mirror glassed,
Shape something of that weird a fairy eye
    Reads in the prophet-book of time;
    And in low lullabies of rhyme
    Whisper them the fate discerned
    In the page for them new-turned—
For, while the merry midnight chime
        Rang clear and high,
The old year perished utterly
And a new era came to men.
    Ah! we fairies count not years;
    Laughing see we Time depart,

We are as we were ;
But men follow him with tears.
Ah ! we have no deadened heart,
Feeble strength, and furrowed brow,
Marking off the weary Now
From the better Then.
No long, foreseeing fears,
No restless hopes, no doubts of change to grow,
Vex *us* with a futurity of care :
No dull regrets, no keen incessant woe,
Vex *us* from the old years past by,
No bitter memory.
Nought nought of these we know,
Save from the cry
Wrung from the children of humanity.
But they ! Their fitful life
Is fretted with uneven change,
Waxing and waning, creeping, rushing on,
Wavering through its narrow range,
Lulled by love and chafed with strife,
Gloomed with shade and glad with light,
With the smiles of Heaven made bright,
Darkened by Hell's malison.

So runs for men the round of years :
What marvel then that each new date
Wakes them to war of hopes and fears,
To anxious questionings of fate?

Ah ! could they know, as we can know,
In signs and voices of the night
When one year comes and one must go,
What chances wait for them, what woe,
What love, what hatred, what delight !
But they are not given sight
Of anything to-morrow brings;
They hear no sound of coming things.
And we fairies warn in vain,
For we may not tell them plain,
And their grave wits are too slow
To catch the fleeting sense of dreams.
Yet come, on noiseless wings,
Soft and silent as the beams
Creeping through the blinded pane,
Through the hushed rooms flit stealthily
Waking in the sleep-locked eye
Golden glowing shadowings
Of what shall happen bye and bye.
Murmur by the sleeper's ear
An undulating melody
Very sweet and low :
Sing it softly till he hear
Softly through his rest,
Till it vaguely touch the sense
He wots not of in his own breast,
Slumbrous, mole-eyed prescience,
And he see the far off near

In a visionary show.
    But be the dream
With as little darkness as it may;
Let the bright all brightness seem,
Let the blackness pale away,
Let sorrow wait for sorrow's day.

And what of sadness should be for him,
    The scarce four-wintered boy?
    Even his sleep is joy.
In baby grace of rounded limb
    Beautiful he lies:
His little head, thrown back, just dints
The tiny arm that glints
In the moonlight like smooth pearls
Through the pale gold of the curls
Tossed backwards from his fair flushed cheeks;
    The blue darkness of his eyes
Shades through their fringed lids' opal lucent white;
The half-closed mouth is happy with a smile.
So sleeps he still and doubtless dreams the while,
    Of the evening's glee,
    And how the wondrous tree
Bore Christmas fruit of toys and baubles bright:
For see one small hand slumber-wandering seeks
The mimic watch, too dear to lay aside,
With scarlet ribbons round his fair throat tied,
    And o'er his head,

Mid the white flutings of his little bed,
Glitters the nursery warrior's new-won pride,
The harmless sword at whose flashed blade
His mother and his nurse will seem afraid,
  And, struck at flying, mimic pain
  Till he kiss them well again.
As thou dreamest now so dream on, fair boy,
  Dream of thy happy play;
Little thy mirth has now of alloy,
  Let the night but image the day.
Dream, fair boy, of thy mother's eyes
  Looking such love on thee,
And thy father's merry mimicries
  As he gallops thee on his knee.
Dream of thy fresh child wonder at life,
Dream of the sweet surprise
In every hour of thy being rife,
  Now when all things are new,
  And the face of earth and the heavens' blue
And the daily form of common things
  In thy young mind discerned
Come with the joy of imaginings
  And the freshness of things new learned.
So baby dream till, morning-eyed,
  Thou laugh to be awake, and play
  Thy cunning trick of every day
Sly clambering to thy mother's side.

And she oh what shall her dreamings be?
Let her dream of the merry days when she,
Spoiled pet of the house that welcomes her now
With the quiet of matron cares on her brow,
Frolicked away her careless hours,
Vexing the house with pranks like ours
When our merry malice was high,
Laughing and teasing, yet loving most;
   And her startled eye
The wrath from the heart of the chider wiled,
For the lips that scolded her smiled.
And there was not the lightest care to press
On her heart as she danced her way,
Pure and light as a sunborn ray,
In her heart and her life a happy child,
  Only a woman in loveliness.
   Let her dream how he came,
And the mirth of her laugh was no more the same;
  And yet he came but to bless.
Let her dream how he waked into life
  The woman that slept in her;
Let her dream how he whispered "wife,"
And childhood had no more bliss,
  And all her heart was astir,
And she knew her for ever his.
   Then let her dream
She has floated calmly along life's stream,
  A many days' journey, far ahead,

And she sees in her own her mother's face,
        Her mother who is dead;
And her husband's brow bears time's wrinkled trace,
And there are grizzles of grey in his hair,
And he walks with an old man, sober air,
        But his eyes have the same fond look;
        And their love seems yet to spread
Though stiller, more wide and more deep,
As the many-voiced eager brook
Deepens and widens towards the bay,
Though it moves with a calmer sweep
        And hushes its happy lay.
And, very rich in love and trust,
They sit together on an Old Year's night
And round them in young faces' light
        See the fair memory of their own
                In the years by flown;
And hear the New Year's plans discussed,
        Their children's buoyant schemes;
And, young in heart through so much love,
        Talk youthful thoughts on youthful themes,
        Scarce feeling that themselves are old,
Scarce noting how the days remove
From the days when they could say
        "Next year and next," nor be too bold.
                Thus be her dreams.
        But what shall sleep unfold
        To him, her husband? For the heart
Of a man busy with his part

In the turmoil of life's fray,
Cares not with far thoughts to stray
From the story of to-day :
The anxious eager Now is more
Than long futures, days before.
Tell him if the work in hand
Shall go fitly, as he planned ;
Has he gained a step or so
On the onward upward way ?
Show him, tell him, yea and yea.
Then, while his visions bring the glow
Of worthy-won success to him,
Let *hers* a portion of them grow :
Let him all the while
See her fond triumphant smile,
See her blue eyes happy dim
With the dear kind tears.
Let him seem to lead her through the busy years,
Busy years with strength and labour happy and astir,
Let him taste twice sweeter pleasure
In won honours, in won treasure,
Because he worked for her.

Leave them in sweet rest, pass by
To the quiet chamber where
Loving in locked arms they lie,
Whitely draped and blossom fair,

Like fresh flowers amid the snows:
Both beautiful in beauty most apart,
White snowdrop and glad rose.
Ah ! we might weep,
Watching your maiden sleep,
Sweet strangers, sister-linked in heart,
To know how He draws nigh,
The severer whom ye cannot fly.
But now we will not make you sad
With the sorrow that shall be.
Sleep on, fair snowdrop, pure and white
As calm St Lucy in the hall
To whom thy lover likens thee,
Sleep, and in dreams be glad.
Look how the chestnut-blossoms fall
Where the spring-breeze flickers light,
Along the budding avenue,
And village children, two and two,
Laden with spring-flowrets strew
The path before thy feet:
And thou art coming by his side
Back to thy love's home, his bride:
And the voice of welcome is sweet:
And she who now to thy side is pressed,
With only the look of love in her face,
Welcomes thee best,
Thy sister then by a dearer tie—
But dream not for how short a space.

Ah ! must the red rose die ?
Alas ! sweet rose that art so budding bright,
    So joyous fair,
Wailings for thee will vex the summer night,
    Thou lying there
In a great stillness, motionless and white,
Calm in the dreamless quiet of the dead.
    Hush ! she turns her head
With a little sigh, as though heart-oppressed :
    We vex her rest
With dim forebodings that work but pain.
    Sweet let them fade from thy brain,
    Fold thee to shadowless slumber again.
Dream not, we will not shape for thee
    Visions of young delight,
Lest to the things that be
    Love-links clasp thy soul too tight.
Dream not, but rest in quiet deep
    Close folded to her side,
    Thy loved, thy brother's bride,
Who breathes e'en now his name in sleep.

Does he breathe thine, white snowdrop ? Doubt it not.
    Do ever his day-dreams leave out thee
In their cloud-limnings of his coming lot ?
    And truly how should it be
We could whisper promise of joy to his heart
Where thou his best joy shouldst have no part ?

                   11

Nay but swiftly to him we fly
Where he sleeps in the turret-chamber nigh,
And we picture thee to his happy eyes,
Moving through all his destinies.
We show him the purpose fulfilled
Which thou hast helped him to frame,
And the honour ye both have willed
His by the noble claim
Of one who, with a manly might
Strained for his brethren to the most
In all brave cause of truth and right,
Has made fair prisoner of fame,
With not one fleck of shame for cost.
Let him seem to stand
Amid a great sea by his whisper stirred,
A whirl of men all eager on his word,
Himself possessed by his own earnestness.
Let him seem to hear
In the great council of the land
The sudden hush his eloquence confess,
The pleasant voice of praise
Buzz "Is not this a man of heart and hand,
A man among the men of modern days?"
But let her low voice in his ear
Ring more dearly,
Ring more clearly,
Ring through sweet clearness all above,
One with his conscience, one with his own pride,

And sweet, oh trebly sweet with love.
Dream on, young lover, dream thy dream of life
   All rainbow dyed,
And, in the golden centre, picture her thy wife.

Gently, oh yet more gently here:
  This sleeper's face is sad,
There clings to the lash one lingering tear—
   Why did it spring?
  Did she weep because many were glad
  To-night in their happy gathering
  With the wealth of love sympathies,
   And she felt so lone?
  Did she weep, who was once so gay
   In her girlhood long agone,
  That her youth has withered away
  And the light is dulled in her eyes
  And fretted lines have vexed her brow
  And the golden hair is deadened with grey
  And no long looks rest on her now?
   She is beautiful no more.
  "She is old" they say "she is old,"
  And her heart within her grows cold,
   Learning the cruel lore.
And doubtless she, musing alone to-night
When the music and dances were o'er,
  Looked on the ghosts of the buried years,
And moaned in her heart for their love and their light,

Lost love and lost light,
Till she rested in tears
From the sorrowful labour of thinking.
And how could she knit her being again
To hers whom she saw with the ghosts of time,
Knit her to her with a broken chain,
A lapse in its golden linking?
And how read the poem of former days
In the newer's saddened paraphrase,
When the music of measure and rhyme
Has died from the strain?
Hush! that was an angel passing us.
There did no voice speak,
But there did come to her
A comfort messenger,
Telling her how to seek
The shattered links, the vanished melody.
How was it? Ah! the meaning is too high:
We fairies have in these heaven-thoughts no part.
But was it not something thus,
"That through much loving she should find a bliss
In all things loved and loving on the earth,
And have the fullness of its beauty in her heart"?
Is herein any mirth,
To have her love in love which is not hers,
Her joy in joy which other bosoms miss?
Alas! we cannot fathom this.
But we know how to gladden her sleeping.

She shall see how on her way
Many bless her, many say
"'Tis her gift to make care less,"
And the happy bring her their happiness,
And she comforts the souls of the weeping.
And she shall wander in her dreams
Through haunts as fair as ours,
Shall feel the joy of sunny gleams,
As we feel it when they pass
Through green leaves in golden streams
Slanting to the shadowed grass,
Feel the quick delight of flowers:
And in gladness at the beauty she shall bless
Her Maker that she is and earth has loveliness.

Sir Hugh sleep sound to-night:
He will sleep more sound, ere next winter be gone,
Beside his wife 'neath the sculptured stone
Where she and his firstborn have waited him long.
Well, he looks hale and strong;
But 'tis many a year since his hair turned white,
And there gathers a clouding over his sight,
And his limbs grow soon weary of any toil.
Age has his life for spoil.
And he will not tremble to see strong Death
Snatch from her withered clutch the prey.
"I am old, my children," often he saith,
"It cannot be long ere I go my way,

And be no more seen.
And I think you will sorrow, and truly I
Shall be loth at heart to bid you good-bye.
    But I trow I have truly had my day, ·
A long and a happy day on the whole,
    As little cumbered with grief and teen
As well may chance to a human soul.
        And now I ween
That life and I must soon weary each other,
    Who already are grown each to each something
        cheap.
Well, we shall part as friends should do,
    Go thy way, kind life, though a man should
        not weep,
There's a sigh for thy sake from thy gossip Hugh,
    As thou turnest from him and he from thee.
    So we two shall good-bye it—soon, may be.
What then, dear children, has not your brother,
    The bright merry boy that was firstborn and best,
Gone before me by twenty-five years?
    And she has been seven years now at her rest,
Whom I rarely speak of for fear of tears:
Yes, seven years now since we lost your mother.
    And surely 'tis time for me as well,
    Time that the even funeral bell
Should usher me forth at the old hall-gate,
Should usher me forth to join them who wait,
        Wife and son."

So saith Sir Hugh, but he cannot foresee
Where two are waiting shall wait him three.
    Doth he guess of his rose's doom?
       Red rose, so sweet and wild,
        Withered in its bloom,
       Bright face, so sweet that smiled,
        Decaying in the tomb,
        Death won.
  So in his dreaming let him not hear
       Her voice calling,
    Though it be so dear.
But let the murmur low and clear,
      Like hill echoes falling,
  Of the two beloved who rest,
      Come to him very sweet—
"Hasten, beloved and best,
Fold thy wife to thy breast,
Take thy boy's hand in thine,
Say to us 'ye are mine.'
      Oh beloved, it is time we should meet."
Yea let him hear their voices and the voices
      That were lost
  From his merry boyish time,
  From his busy manhood's prime,
     Those he loved most,
Calling him till he in the thought rejoices
    That death might mend life's broken links.
Call him, call him, in their voices

Till he sinks,
Dreams he sinks in the outstretched arms
Waving him home,
Feels in their clasp no doubtings, no alarms,
Knowing they do but carry him home.
Call him, call him, in their voices;
He can hear us now in his sleep,
But he will not hear, it will be so deep,
His sleep in the earth, ere the next year come.

Fairies, the moon has risen so high
That St Lucy in the hall
Is surely uncrowned of her moonbeam crown,
And never a ray can fall
To the panoplies in the archway down
Nor in broken lights on the hollies lie,
And the crystal sparkling of the pane
Must have dulled into dead frost again.
But yet a little foot of the sky
Has the climbing moon to go
Ere she reach her topmost place.
And fair is the omen that we have stood
By every child of our favoured race
Resting within the home to-night
Ere she have dropped from her airy height
To the lap of the waters below.
Else had it verily boded small good
To the fortunes of this line,

And the valley fay had risen weeping—
    She who by her love church-blessed
    Of human nature grew possessed,
     And human death, and human rest
      Guarded by the holy shrine—
Had risen ghostly from the deep grave's keeping,
    Wringing shadow hands, and sobbing
      For a nearing day
When the blessing should have passed away,
And the honour dwindled to decay,
      And the name's last stay,
     Last in whose veins was throbbing
The blood of Amys flushed with hers,
     Should be lying
     Under alien skies,
     Staring out of glassy eyes
At the dark-robed ministers
    Death-missioned to the dying,
     Should be lying
    Dying, name and race so dying.

But now let the long years cycle on
Till their two dark centuries be gone,
    And the new year's moon again
Touch, at that self-same hour,
That self-same spot of sky, and look
     Down where they stood,
She and the knight, by the running brook

Thawed by the yesterday's rain :
And her brow was dewed by the christening
shower
And sained by the sign of the holy rood,
And her hand unclasped The Book
That yields to no evil might,
And she read the holy name
No evil tongue can read aright,
While new being on her came,
And a soul of human kind,
And her elfin nature passed
To the dead years left behind—
Left behind
As the moon left the shadow o'er her cast
And swept on proudly through the free blue air ;
And yet the soft deep cloud was very fair,
Did the moon not linger at last ?
And yet our elfin life is very sweet,
Turned she not once and again
To look back on us and all she had left,
While her bare white feet
Slowly the waves of the chill brook cleft,
As she crossed to the other side ;
And we were calling her back in vain,
For she loved him more.
Turned she not once and again,
Even in his caressing ?
Was there not in her joy a little pain

For all, and us, she had left?
  But she crossed to the other shore.
Gone! gone! our gold-haired valley fay.
Gone! gone! our fairest whom we loved.
Onwards with him, along the homeward way,
With a woman grace she moved.
  Gone, gone, our valley fay!
But the bride of Amys was more than woman
      fair,
Pure in heart and happy-minded, whom to love was
      love's best blessing:
He would say "My true wife, Lucy, God was for me
      on the day
When I heard the clear voice singing through the
      sweet and summer air."

  What? Are some among us here
    New come from fair Britanny,
  Or from tending on the King
  In Avilion's mystic isle
    Where he watches musingly
  In his mirror's shadowing
    How the things of time go by
  Day by day, and year by year,
  Nothing changed for him the while
  Till the fulfilling of the fate be o'er
  And he come once more
    To his second destiny—

Some new come among us here
 Who have never heard the tale
How Sir Amys, on a summer-morn,
 Riding out a hawking through the vale,
  Paused to hear the singing
  Of a sweet voice silver ringing,
   As it were
From the greenness of a thorn,
  Making music of the air,
  Making music of his heart?
And he said "Since I was born
  Never heard I song like this,
  Making me of it a part,
  Making me as one with bliss."
Then he sprang from off his steed,
  And he hunted, hunted vainly,
  Though he heard the voice still plainly
  Trilling out the wondrous song.
"Here" he cried "is none indeed!
  Yet I hear the wondrous song
   Still more plainly.
I might hear it so for ever, never thinking time
  grew long."
So he came there day by day, living almost in the
  singing
  Of the sweet voice silver ringing
  From the arbour of the thorn.

"Oh! might I see thee!" he would say, "thee won-
　　derful who singest so."
Then the voice would seem to mock him, trilling
　　out a laughing scorn,
Else would pass away in sweetness, dying in a ca-
　　dence slow,
　　　Dying, dying, sweet and slow.
Never might he see the singer, though he hunted
　　far and near
While the summer-weeks passed onwards setting all
　　the flowers aglow,
Till when August's scorching breath was hot upon
　　the yellowed corn,
He, leaning 'gainst the sloping thorn-tree, listening,
　　thrilled throughout to feel
All the strangeness and the sweetness of the lay
　　that rose so clear,
And, through the exceeding sweetness, sadness waken-
　　ed in his heart,
　　　Trembled in a tear.
"Ah!" he sighed "and this that singeth doubtless
　　hath but its brief part
In the lifetime of this earth, hath no share in Hea-
　　ven's weal.
Ah the pity! Ah the pity!" Then from his mist-
　　clouded eye
　　　Dropped the trembling tear.

It glistened on a white white hand
    Gleaming suddenly,
Where among the grass it lay,
    Where she lay
    Who rose suddenly like a dream,
Our beautiful, the valley fay.
    "Now" she said "what is this spell
I cannot understand?
      Did God teach it thee?
    That warm dewdrop when it fell
      Laid a charm on me;
    When it touched me it did seem
To sink into my heart and swell—
Scarce is there room within my breast,
    Is thy dewdrop there still?
      Will it not rest?
See thou hast won thy will,
    I am made manifest,
Speak to me now and tell me what this is."
    But he answered, "Nay I know not, it may be
My sadness, moving thee who art a thing of bliss,
    Has touched a spring in thee
To link thee closer to my human kind and make
A power in me new life in thee to wake."

So she questioned through the summer-day,
Till the evening darkened slowly grey

And the white stars shone above;
     So he made replies;
  Thinking in his heart the while
    "She is too fair
To look on and not love.
She is more worthy love than tongue can
    say,
    Were the soul but there,
  She, with her pureness free from guile,
Her laughter and her phantasies:
And she has St Lucy's eyes
    With their innocent fearless smile;
As they look above the shrine
    Set in the minster's southern aisle,
So hers gaze in mine
With a childishness half divine.
    She is too innocent
    To look on and not love."
    And long before he went,
  When the white stars shone above
And the night spread darkling o'er the sky,
    In his inmost heart he wist
That they were thenceforth spirit-nigh,
Knit by a mystic sudden tie,
    Some strange tie of heart to heart
    Between two lives so far apart,
    He a mortal, she a mist.

Lingering homewards with a musing pace
    Through the dusky avenue,
Thinking of her pure pale face,
Thinking of her heedless grace,
    In the still air Amys knew
Voices following him along
    In a far faint song,
        "Choose now thy way;
Love her for ever or leave ·her to-day,
Love her for ever or else let her be
        As nothing to thee."
Voices following him along
In a far faint answering song,
    "He will not leave her, his love is too new,
        And the choice is made.
    He will not leave her, and we are afraid
        For our sister's sake :
For the strong love-will of a man can make
    Fairies love as his mortals do,
And, loving, they can learn to weep,
And, weeping, learn to sleep death's sleep,
From which fairies cannot wake.
    Amys, Amys, be thou true.
If thou snap the mystic tie
    Of heart to heart between the two,
She or thou must die.
        Be true, be true,
Lest thine own life should be at stake."

And eyes, St Lucy's eyes, *her* eyes, did seem
To look on him as out of some old dream.
And it was borne upon his heart
     As though One said
   "He will not leave her, his love is too high,
     And the choice is made.
But oh Amys, do thy part
In strength and honour, lest she die
And gain no human likeness save to die."

Fairies will ye hear the rest?
    Hear how Amys day by day
    Wooed the gold-haired valley fay,
Till there glimmered in her breast
    That strange human glow
      We do not know,
And her loving was confessed
Mid her peals of silver laughter
And her moods of merry freaks
And her passions of delight
And her sudden anger's height
Flushing redly through her cheeks,
And her seeming cold disdain
And the bright smiles blushing after
As she laughed love back again.
     "Love" she said "since love is pleasure
I must love thee, love, to-day,
    Love perchance a merry morrow;

So many days have passed away,
    And I not weary of my treasure."
But he said " Canst love but so ?
    Ah! so often love is sorrow ;
Canst thou no such loving know ?
    Dear this of thine no loving is,
    It is but loving loving's bliss—
Well, 'tis thy best, love even so."
    And it vexed his longing much
    That an unseen bar seemed ever
        Them to sever,
    And he might not feel her touch,
        And her face
    Died to air before his kiss,
    And his arms, stretched to embrace,
Closed on only nothingness ;
    While he saw her standing nigh,
    Mocking him with melody,
    Laughters for his every sigh,
She in all things sorrowless.
    But ever in the twilight falling
        O'er the darkening avenue,
    Still he heard our voices calling,
        Calling " Be thou true
            Lest thou die,"
        Saw the deep eyes earnestly
        Looking " Be thou true
            Lest she die."

Will ye listen a little longer?
    The moon is yet on high.
    Will ye hear how sorrow came,
    When the summer had gone by
And love had grown deeper and stronger
    But sad with a fear and a shame?
    For the priest said "Son, this is sin.
Wilt thou peril thy soul alive
    The love of this being to win
    Whom God has not thought worthy love
But given her part with the Devil?
        What! and art thou so wroth!
    Yea now, though thou shouldst prove
Her free from the power of evil,
    As thou wilt fondly believe,
Still it were sin to wive
    With this elf creature nought akin
To Christian people. What but woe
        Were there in the tie for both?
She must see thee die, and know
Never ye should meet again:
    Dying, thou must sorely grieve
She for ages should remain
Leading an existence vain
    To die at last in nothingness,
If she 'scape that endless pain
    Thou wilt not hear of for her meed.

My son ! and how should Heaven bless,
Or the Church take to her embrace,
Thy strange unhallowed elfin race?
Living without hope or creed,
Dying as the brute beast dies,
Dread will be their destinies."
Then the heart of Amys grew all grief,
While he listened daily to the cruel word.
"Cruel," he said "is thy word,
Stabbing me, like a quick-edged sword,
Deep, deep, into my heart:
But never think to make in me belief
That she is aught of ill."
Yet he answered, being sore bested,
"Priest and teacher thou art
To show us the path to tread;
Thou knowest God's will,
Therefore to thy rule I bow.
God help me now!"

The moon is low, is sinking low,
But she is not paling yet:
There is still a while ere she set,
And a longer while ere the shrill cock crow
For the cold grey winter morn.
Will ye tarry to hear the end?
Hear how Amys wearily must wend
To the leaf-stripped thorn

In whose greenness they did meet:
And the autumn wind moaned his despair
        Ever and anon
    Back to him in long shrill moans,
    Beat the brook against its stepping stones
    Till it answered too in moans,
Shook the shivering boughs more bare
    Till they answered too in moans;
And the dank dead leaves hissed 'neath his feet;
        And the rain plashed on
    With a sorrowful sound;
    And bitter voices in the air
        Moaned around
    "Can he love unsay?
    Too late, too late to-day.
    He has loved her life away,
        Now she will die.
        Let him teach her to die."
And Amys bowed his head
In shame and sorrow very dread,
Yet he went on, remembering
The word he spake unto the priest;
    But he gasped, like one dying, for breath.
He cried "Oh saints! this is a bitter thing.
And I fare forth to a merry tryst!
    For me much better were death.
But I thank God she will suffer least,
    Since by her nature she cannot sorrow.

Mayhap for the day she will anger and pine,
But the eyes that smile into mine
And the lips I have never kissed
  Will smile gaily again to-morrow."
 He cried "And I, am I false? but ye know,
  Spirits that mock me, my truth
   By the depth of my woe.
Ye know that love from my life cannot go,
  Though I willed it so,
Since now the love has become one with me ;
  And I hate my youth
That it must give me such terrible might
  To suffer and yet be strong with life—
   Years, and years, and years,
  All with this deadly bitterness rife—
   To suffer and yet be strong with life."
And the voices cried " Thou sayest right,
   So will it be.
   Years, and years, and years,
  All with this deadly bitterness rife,
  To suffer and yet be strong with life."
   But he went on wearily;
And the wind moaned and moaned more drearily;
And the brook and the boughs moaned more drearily;
And the rain plashed in chiller showers.
  But the pure eyes that watched him oftentimes
   Smiled on him as through tears :
  And a sweet voice, more sweet than ours,

Fell with a music as of vesper chimes,
"Now, through all thy sorrow, be thou strong,
Choosing any anguish more than wrong.
God judgeth, God giveth aid—
Shrink not from the duty on thee laid."
So it sighed away in sadness, as he passed
Along the vale and saw her near,
With her head aside his coming foot to hear,
Beneath the black bare thorn,
With her arm clasped round it fast,
With a new look in her eyes,
Half sorrow half surprise.
"Love" she said "I seemed to be so lorn,
Waiting longingly for thee.
Wilt thou drive away
The spell that is on me to-day?
What is it? Is it pain?
Long ago I used to laugh to see
The wild wind tear the red leaves from the tree
And whirl them so high,
And I chased them as it chased.
Long ago I laughed to catch the rain
With my palms for goblets placed.
Now my heart is vexed
For the poor leaves that die.
Now it irks me to see the stripped earth lie
So shelterless and waste,
Bare to the bleak black sky;

And my mind is perplexed
With wonder, almost as if I had done
With this fairy life of mine
As bright and as light as spray in the sun,
And had grown to that strange life of thine,
The weary life of the weary world.
Love, laugh with me, make me merry again."
But he turned from her, saying no word,
And in a passionate outburst hurled
Him face to earth and wept
With a man's fierce anger of grief.
But she never stirred.
Stone-like, with tight hands together pressed,
In a mute amaze she kept
Watching still and wonderingly;
Till at length she said "Is this grief?
It seems more than the pain of things that die;
For they grow quiet as if they slept.
Now, though I love him best,
I would he had loved, not me,
But a woman; for she would have known
If any could give him relief.
And I would now that I could sorrow as he,
That he might not bear it all and alone."
Then she crept
Timidly near to him and more near:
And there seemed no bar between them now:
And she stooped and kissed his brow,

Saying "Let me mourn as thou."
Then she seemed to shiver with a sudden fear
And a sudden pang:
And we saw how the quick human tears upsprang,
And she wept as women weep.
Then he started, as if from sleep,
And he felt her touch, and he felt her kiss,
And he clasped her close to his breast,
Who never had lain there yet,
And her cheeks with his tears and hers were wet;
And the tears seemed to sink
Down to her heart till it gasped oppressed
With a sorrow half like bliss
Because it was a part of his;
And closer and closer the mystic link
Seemed knitting to his her being.
He cried "And how can I think
I of a coward .fleeing?
To leave thee, owning my loving a sin,
Calling thy loving a moment's and vain,
Now when thou hast grown to my being akin,
Only through love."
But softly from above
Rang that strange voice, slow and plain,
"Not through love only;
Was there not sorrow?"
But we cried ever
"Nay why should ye part for one to live lonely

And one to die?
Take heed to thee Amys; the day ye shall sever
One of the two may lie dead on the morrow.
Take heed to thyself; if her love goes by
She cannot die."
But the voice rose clear above our song
"Yet be strong,
Choosing any anguish more than wrong."
Then he rose up, very white, and said
"Dearest never think of me again;
Let it be as if I were dead,
And do not try to learn our human pain,
Who canst not our human comfort know.
Laugh, love, like thyself, and say good bye.
Love, I must no more look on thy dear face;
Give me one little kiss and let me go."
But she made a little startled cry,
Like a baby child amazed
At a sudden chiding blow,
And into his eyes she gazed
With a fond beseeching grace,
Saying "Love it is not true?
Thou art mocking me.
Let be, let be, with the idle jest,
Take back my hands, lay my head on thy breast."
Saying "Is it because it seems to thee
That I cannot love as a woman might do?
But teach me then, I shall learn the way

Easily, easily, after to-day:
    For have I not wept thy tears?"
Saying "Is it because I cannot share
Thy grave long thoughts as a woman might
    share?
But, love, I can charm from thee all life's care,
    And make thee one gladness of all life's years.
    Oh! love me a little while longer yet,
    Oh! a little little while longer yet."
Then his frame with a great trembling shook,
    And his teeth were set,
And the words he gasped died away,
Like the cries of a dreamer in the night,
    In a stifled moan.
Then he looked in her eyes with a weary look,
And at last we could hear him say—
    Oh his lips were white,
And his eyes were strange with a cold hard light,
    And his voice was dull and slow—
    "Now it may not be.
But kiss me again ere I go,
That I may think of thee
As even in farewell my own,
    Even in this farewell."
And she clung to him and kissed him, brow, and
    lip, and cheek,
    And she did not speak,
But piteously and pleading looked up into his face:

But he put her slowly from him, and hurried with
    an angry pace
Homeward through the dreary valley, in the ever
    darkening rain:
      And a shadow fell
Over the thorn, and the loud long winds hissed
    through the shivering dell.

      Is the moon there yet?
      She grows pale and chill
    In a waning gleam;
      But she has not set,
      And the house is still.
    Listen while men yet dream.
Faint grew his heart, faint with a long distress,
    And like a fevered sleep his days lagged by,
And the sad nights passed o'er him slumberless,
    And he was wearier than one like to die.
And in the minster's southern aisle
    We watched him daily, how he spent
Long hours before St Lucy's shrine,
    His gaze upon those pure eyes bent
With their innocent fearless smile
And their childishness half divine,
    Eyes that were also *hers*.
And he prayed " Now thou wilt pardon me,
Thou dear saint, that I gaze on thee
    Longer for the love of one

Who from my chilled life is gone.
Ah! thine eyes that hers are like!
    Surely they were messengers
    Of strength to me in need:
Thine the voice that seemed to strike
    Like God's bidding on my heart.
    And I obeyed.
    I crushed my heart: and now I bleed,
Bleed inly hurt to death.
    Hast thou no aid?"
And once a voice, like a low breath
Of far off music, answering said
    "Well hast thou done thy part:
    Have hope, God giveth aid."

But, when the cold white snow was spread
    Far o'er the earth's numbed breast,
    He said "I know not any rest
Thinking of her: for do I know
Into what change her life might grow,
    She being changed through me?
And what if she does not forget?
    Ah! it may be that she
Is weeping wildly for me yet;
    It may be she is dead."
And pain-damps stood upon his brow;
    He sat in struggle with himself,
His strong hands clenched until the blood

Oozed from the nail-clipped flesh.
Then at length he rose, the master of his mood;
    He said "I will not sin afresh
I will not seek her." Sudden stood,
    Right at his knees, a fire-eyed elf
Shrilling "Brave heart! she must linger alone,
    Dying alone with her misery,
Lest the sight of her pain should quicken thine
        own
        And a cruel word be broken!
Oh, brave Sir Amys! But see, and see,
By my touch and my spell I have glamoured thee.
    Look up, true lover, and see her die.
Look up—Do I keep the word I have spoken?"
    Then Amys wakened by the spell,
    Standing in the shadowed dell
Where he stood that summer-morn
    When on his ears the sweet voice fell
From out the downward sloping thorn;
        And he saw her lie
    With her sinking head half propped
        Against the tree,
    And her lax hands listless dropped,
Hands so thin and worn;
    And her cheek and lips were pale
        As a dying girl's might be
When the change came nigh.
And, one by one, the slow tears crept

Welling out from her closed eyes,
As though she, wearied, only slept
    Dreaming bitter memories.
    And she sighed a low weak wail,
    Like far waves in the sobbing gale
        Sighing along the shore.
And Amys, listening, held his breath,
        Hearing her sigh
"Alas! I would be glad in death
    Might he but come once more,
        Once, only once, before I die."
Then with sudden bounds he sprang
    Upwards, onwards, where she lay;
    Crying "Let doom fall on me,
        So I but her doom retrieve,
So I save her but one pang."
    But, even as he gained the tree,
A whisper through the branches stirred
        And passed away:
    And he was wakened from the spell,
And, in the thorn-tree's shadow, heard
    The music of the far church-bell,
        And knew it was St Lucy's eve.

    Listen again—white grows the moon,
    And keen is the morning's chill,
    The life of the toilers will waken soon,
        And the hurry and din

Of the day begin,
But now they are wrapped in our dream-webs still.
Listen then : even that night,
While Amys sleepless tossed on his bed,
His hot hands pressed to his aching head,
And his eyes in the darkness burning with sight
Of her, her always, now cold and dead
Alone in the snows 'neath the bare black tree,
Now laughing upon him happy and bright
With the old child love and the old child glee,
Now as he saw her that day
Weeping her life away,
Sudden there streamed a light,
A silver glory of light, through the gloom,
And a stillness was in the room;
And his heart grew hushed and at rest.
Then was a white form there,
In the midst of the brightness a brighter ray,
Like the angels fair,
With a pure white star above her brow,
And a pure white lily at her breast,
And in her hand the martyr's bough.
She smiled on him, and her clear eyes
Were like the eyes he loved the best,
But deeper, as the depth of skies,
And solemn with a happy awe
As though they saw
Always Heaven's mysteries :

And Amys knew that these were they,
    Watching him ofttimes in his pain,
Whereon to look seemed as to pray
    And grow more strong in faith again :
And knew the strange sweet voice that spake,
    Saying " Amys, fall not in despair
        For her sake.
Thou mayst give thy life for hers, as was thy
    prayer,
But wait in patience and be strong
    Lest it be granted thee in vain,
And the past bitterness be also all in vain.
To-day I saved thee, but I may not save again
        From the snare.
Now listen : as the year wanes she will wane,
Die with it to the nothingness of air,
Lost like the breath of perfume or of song,
    Except she win another life.
Thou, in the death-hour of the year,
Stand where the valley brook clips round
The thorn-tree copse's fern-fringed bound,
    Call to her, for she will hear,
        ' Thou, if thou wilt be my wife,
    Cross the brook to me, and let
    Thy brow with christening dew be wet,
Sained with symbol of our creed,
    Place thy hand for troth in mine,
So shalt thou have mortal meed,

13

Human life for this of thine
With its wild sweet fairy gladness,
Hope of second life divine
     For thine endless fairy days :
But, if thou dost loath the sadness
     And the darkness of our ways,
And wilt have thy shadeless glee
     Once again among thy fays,
          Choose ; it shall be given thee.'
Yet, oh Amys, know the danger on thy head :
If she choose once more her elfin life to live,
     There is a price to give ;
And when the fated hour is sped
     She will look on thee in her careless mood,
          Thee lying dead,
     With the ignorance of love
     Of her fairy sisterhood
     And light to her old joys will go
Thinking nothing of the dead.
          Canst thou do this ?"
And Amys, in a low voice reverent,
     And sudden with his yearning, spoke
"This I will do as Heaven is."
And from him in a breath the vision went,
     And he knelt praying till the morning broke.

          Did there one stir,
     Awake in the house ?   No all is hushed.

'Twas a gust of wind through the chambers
    rushed.
  The day will be rude.
Yes all is hushed : hear now the last.
And Amys waited in his restless mood,
    And weary at the heart for her:
  And slow, and slow, the grey days passed,
  And ever fear would come to him
    "What and if she die before !"
And his breath came quick, and his sight grew dim,
And a shudder thrilled him from limb to limb,
And he longed to seek her but yet forbore.
And ever the elf was urging him sore—
  (For the riddle from us was hidden
  Of what was granted and what forbidden,
  And we watched in wonder and fear)—
And ever we were crying
    "Haste she is dying :
Haste, she prays only to see thee once more."
And he panted to seek her, but yet forbore.
  But, when the fateful night was come,
    The cold drear death-night of the year,
  He hasted darkling from his home
    Long ere the midnight hour was near,
  And waited by the brook's swelled tide,
  And called, and called, but none replied,
  Till all the clear stars specked the sky
  And the wakened moon was high.

Then he heard
A faint faint voice reply
One low word
"Love I die."
Then he called again "Oh, sweet faint voice,
"Come nearer, answer me."
And he spoke and gave her choice
In the words She bade him say,
Who taught him on St. Lucy's eve.
Then she answered from afar "Love, must it be?
Must I choose between my old glad life and thee?
Alas! in that sad higher world of thine men
grieve,
And I am all aweary of the tears."
And we cried "Stay with us, oh! stay.
Life like ours is far too sweet to leave.
Laughters and music ring through all our merry
endless year,
But sorrow darkens o'er the world's vexed way
And all its love and life are but a day."
"Yet" she said "that love, his love, is more than
ours;
And that life, his life, is more than ours,
Although our length of days out-tell its length of
hours."
She sighed "And yet how shall it be?
For in his weeping world, I think,
My love has need of me."

And, while she wavered, rose once more
    His voice towards us from the brink
"Love hast thou chosen? for the night
    Is close upon its midmost hour:
And, when the sudden bell shall wake
The younger year, thou hast no choice to make.
Thou wilt be as thou wast of yore,
    Thine again thy fairy dower
Of all things beautiful save love,
    Save love that will have passed away."
    . Then she rose—
What was that stirred in the house above?
    High over head
Is a sound of wakers that move,
    Beginning the business of day
Before the long night has fled,
    And the dawning glows
    Redden faintly the winter skies.
    Hark! nearer it grows.
      The house is astir.
    Hence! hence! ere mortal witnesser
    Unbidden on our secret pries.
Hence! hence! our talk is vexed with wakening
    eyes.

Lota.

I.

Born owner of old acres, an old hall,
And wide old woods that made the slopes like hills,
Was Gervase Lester, whom his mother taught
To strut among them masterwise ere yet
His unbreeched limbs were strong enough to take
The lithesomeness of schoolboys. In the grey
Of evening hours till bedtime, when she spent
Her sweet caresses on him and her talk
Was mother-like and childish by the fire,
Instead of fairy tales she'd pleasure him
With vague quaint legends of his ancestors
Scowling or simpering at them from their frames.
It did not harm him—likelier did good :
For afterwards, if Gervase Lester mused
A trifle arrogantly on his grace
Of being born in the appendix to the list
Of these historic Lesters, he recalled
Unconsciously the chime of the dear voice

That told their stories, and of some grave notes
Mixed with the prattle, and he took to heart
How proud his mother meant to be of him
If she had lived to see him ripen out
To the fullblown Lester, and so tried to keep
A something of his likeness to her hopes.
Although, among an eager college clique
Of crude philosophers apt to forget
The answers to the questions in the schools,
Not valuing like the examiners
Mere musty grammar and strait sciences,
But who, to make amends, would show by the hour
How different and wide the scope should be
Of their teachers' teaching, and were overbrimmed
With universal thoughts, he learned to boast
Some creeds and principles which would have made
That mild upholder of despotic rules
And ancient strict observances turn pale
With fear and sorrow for him and look up
To see if each right Lester did not stir
And shudder in his frame.

             The young men talked
Much noble nonsense; many generous schemes
Icarian, whose wings must needs melt off
At the first exposure to the garish sun
Of the world's every day; many beliefs
Most beautiful and rounded every way

To a nice perfectness, as bubbles are ;
And many unbeliefs as beautiful
And just as brittle to the first rough proof;
Many true-based delusions ; many truths
Bottomed on dreams, as the moon seems to rest
On clouds....that fade and still the moon is there.
They hoped, they argued, they denounced, they
        planned—
And all their talk was to their great concern
Of how the world should wag of as much use
As a school-boy's shouts at play. Yet the lad's noise
Inures his throat for speeches bye and bye
When he's a statesman or a barrister
Or has to try if weary pews will hear
Another sermon yet and keep awake :
And the outbursts of these ardent half-fledged minds
Prepare them, possibly, for well poised flight,
For some flight anyhow, and that is more
Than skilful gropings in the mud for food,
Like farmyard webfoots, fat, yet eating more.

Yet, " Let them learn " you'll say, " what learning is
Ere they confute it with their phantasies. "
And you'll say wisely. And in truth they'd find
Their teachers something deeper than they know,
If they had lead and line to sound with. Yet
I'll tell you this my thought: a shallow brook
That frets and brattles on and takes some miles

A little helping moisture for green growths
Is better worth than an opaque still pool,
Quite deep, you're told, below, if you could see,
That feeds a slime of chickweed and a marge
Of mud-weeds round about the hole it fills,
And does no more and keeps its stagnant peace.
I will not thank your dull sage, day by day
Growing denser with new learning, while he sees
The wide world stretched outside the little round
Of his small special science as its rim
To hold it in, measures the proper stretch
Of aspirations as to learn or teach
That same small special science, takes the heights
Of lives by how much they have learned or taught
Of the special science. Let him learn and teach:
He has his sort of use, but I will praise
No sleepy wisdom at whose door life cries
"Awake and let me in," and cries unheard.

Gervase became a great man in his clique.
They told the world so most vociferously;
But the world did not listen much at first.
In after years, when they explained to it
How much he could have done if he had cared,
And would have done if things had happened right,
And partly did and partly planned to do,
The world was more impressed and spoke his name
Complacently, as a proud father boasts

"My youngest son, Sir, a wild selfwilled dog,
Would study or would not just when he chose
And how he chose, or else he would have been
First of his year, prizeman in everything—
Too sharp in fact, ('twixt you and me), to pin
His mind to pedant rules; and so he failed."
And that's as sweet as any kind of fame,
For it awakes no jealousies, and each
Who praises shows his own rare competence
To catch the sparkle in the uncut gem,
Hints too that he himself wears in his sleeve
An uncut gem of genius very like
By which he recognized it; and so praise
Rings roundly out and every one is pleased.

Such honour Gervase had, and, had he died
In the young spring of saptime, would have been
Immortal for at least a score of years.
But he, as if a bulb which you have nursed
For some rare tulip should put forth its spikes
A common useful onion, growing ripe
Betrayed his serviceable worth and kind,
And was, nor poet nor philosopher,
But just a clever eager-hearted man,
With work in him if the world wanted work,
And pleasant music if his friends asked songs.
And so he shed his glory while he passed
What he had been when he was clothed in it;

As lime-buds lose their little rosy wings
By opening out in leafage.

　　　　　　　　　　　　But not yet
Was Gervase Lester sobered from the draught
Of heady praises which his friends frothed out
With their young generous measure, when he came
From doing pilgrimage Childe-Harold-wise—
Carrying albeit no more luscious vice
To help him moralize than vanity :
For he was one who never could believe
In Æsop's midden-cock that scraped up pearls
From the rank filth, and who disdained the smutch
Of all ignoble wallowings.　He came
To take his natural place among the squires,
Full to the lips of theories and schemes,
Art aspirations, steam appliances,
The poor made rich by schooling, the rich wise
By unlearning what they've learned and going back
To nature's simpler lessons, the tight straps
Of form and custom loosed from each man's girth,
The landlords governing paternally
And seeing that the girls were taught to sew—
Hopes views and facts, all jumbled contra-wise,
Like the housewife's touzle-bag of sewing silks,
From which each several thread may be drawn out
Perfect and put to use, but which, in the whole,
Seems an unpurposed tangle of clipped shreds.

But the squires would not work with him, did good
In a plain charitable way, or else
Let well alone, or maybe ill alone;
And wondered how a man who rode to hounds
So pluckily as Lester, got that craze
For newfangled social problems, reasoning
By system like a shallow foreigner;
And baited him with friendly dinner-wit
He thought as solid and as savourless
As their traditionary entrées...or,
(As he irreverently dared to think),
Their proper-mannered comely wives and girls.

At last he grew too weary of the squires,
Jokes, dinners, wives, and comely girls; perhaps
Of the reforms and works on his estate,
Which always somewhere crooked from his design.
He'd live awhile in town.   And, half ashamed,
He thought of friends there: one he called his aunt,
His mother's distant cousin, had half made
A son of him by kindness.   Sooth to say
He feared she planned a nearer motherhood:
She had daughters, and one of them, Evelyn,
Stately and simple, with deep quiet eyes
Like sky, blue sky seen through a thin grey cloud,
And a fairness which made beauty of itself,
Had seemed so loveable that still he mused

How strange he had not loved her, and in truth
Had found it hard to keep from telling her
He loved her though he did not. And his aunt
(I'll call her so as he did) had been prompt
To help him past his wish, and Evelyn
Had learned to drop her eyes so suddenly
When he looked at her that he could not help
A pleasure and a shame at once. No blame
That could be shaped lay with him; not a word
Nor sign of suitorship had perjured him;
But yet he felt that there had somewhere lurked
A touch of falseness in him to the girl,
And gladly would have heard that she was wed
And happy.

    For she was to him more dear
Than any woman of the whole wide world:
Only he said "Now I could never love her:" .
Since he had felt those pleasant woman wiles
Of which most Englishwomen fail, the charm
Of bright caprice, subtle simplicities,
Pert bird-like confidence, and kitten ease,
And changing fluent speech of word and look
And pretty sudden gestures, or the charm
Of southern languorous quiet waking up
Into a flash of fire. Then too, because
The foreign women's manners, trimmed to rules
Different from those which wearied him at home,

Had the sweet of strangeness for him, he, who loathed
Our social bugbear that makes wild birds tame
By clipping wings that were designed to fly,
Conventionality, took them to be
More frankly living, less conventional
Than the women drudging on at morning calls
And being civil placidly by rote
In England, where he had seen enough to know
What necessary clockwork fills the place
Of the pith of nature scooped out of their lives
By careful teachers. "I would liefer set"
He thought, "some rare white statue in my house
And talk my heart to it, than one of these
Our proper well-trained damsels, same and good,
Who would not even *look* as if she'd life
Enough to long to live. My statue would,
And would change her beauty with each changing light,
Instead of varying, as my wife would do,
Her ribbons and her roses to one face."
So he still thought "Not Evelyn, she is good,
And very fair, and very lofty souled,
But she is spoiled with training, as we spoil
All sweet frank natures of our English girls.
Let me have innocent wild carelessness,
And the fresh freedom of a natural growth."

And yet did he say wisely? The vine boughs
Which, pruned and trimmed, are stripped of half
      their grace.

Are those that bear rich grapes, not the wild sprays
That droop and twine and wander with the winds,
Growing towards the sunlight as they will.

The home in London chosen, himself installed,
Gervase half eager, half reluctant, went
To greet the Westlands.   Scoldingly the aunt,
And cordially, gave welcome; as one scolds
A truant favourite and praises him
For coming back at last.   The daughters teased,
Evelyn among them, with a playful show
Of making him a stranger, and were kind
With a benevolent modest courtesy......
Which Gervase quite forgot to think by rule,
Although, in sooth, they would have been the same
To one less liked.   But he discerned in them
A frank goodwill, and was at ease, assured
Of his familiar place with them again.
And if sweet Evelyn flushed a little more
Than her sisters when she spoke, it might be chance,
Or else her fairer skin which showed the glow
Sooner than theirs; for she betrayed no sign
Of flutter or of coyness.

                              She had passed
From girl to woman, and was lovelier,
As the evening star grows lovelier, that glows
With its full light, than when it first awoke,

White and uncertain, in its younger gleam.
But she was yet a girl in years, and kept
A something of the child in her grave eyes,
And the child's questioning look. He could not keep
From watching her, she was so rare a thing:
And presently it seemed as if his talk
Was all for her, whoever questioned him
Or answered. And she, by degrees, became
More silent than her share, checked by the sense
Of a half-sweet constraint, and blushed confused
Because he made her beauty present to her.

So Gervase sat and told his travel tales,
Not ill content to be a hero, pleased
With the girls' eager questions and the praise
And half-approving blames of his good aunt,
And Evelyn's quiet smiles. He took amiss
The break, when suddenly a gipsy face,
A quaint face, olive, but with hair all glow,
Like sunshine on brown rivers, crowning it,
Peeped in behind the door, and Constance called
"Lota come in," and, giving sudden chase,
Brought her among them, ruffled and half-cross—
A lithe slight creature, looking scarcely more
Than a girl-grown child; with a rebellious pout,
And a sort of sudden fitful prettiness
Which flickered and died out by moments. "This"
Said Mrs Westland, "is my ward and niece,

14

Whose name is Lota." Gervase, having made
His reverence and noticed the quick grace
Of Lota's answering movement, asked "But I?
Am I to call her Lota? for you give
No other name." But Lota, with her cheeks
A vivid painful crimson, answered him
In lofty fashion, slowly. "I am called
Miss Deveril." He bowed and let her be:
She did not please him; though she instantly
Spoke with a kindness in her voice and eyes
"I would not have attempted that vain flight
If I had known 'twas you. My cousins speak
As if you were a friend." And Ethel laughed,
And said "Moreover Lota knows, alas!
That she cannot, with all her hermit ways,
Escape from meeting you at last, and so
She plucks her nettle boldly." Gervase smiled
"Miss Deveril is kind then to forgive
The nettle for upspringing in her path,"
And that was all. At night, when he sat still
Beside his dying fire, his dreaming sense
Was filled with Evelyn, whose fair sweet face
Would come uncalled; and, if he thought at all
Of Lota, it was as a cross-grained sprite
Unsociable perversely, but not shy,
Who seemed beside calm gracious Evelyn
The olive that gives zest to generous wine.

But he saw Lota more—a score of times—
And then she seemed to him the veriest witch
That ever glamoured men against their wills.
He could not read her. She seemed made to sit
Out of the wind and sing, to play with life,
And think in treble laughters; yet at times,
Rarely indeed, she'd sit in languid rest,
Drooping and limp, and answer with a voice
That seemed asleep and sad; and often too
Stole through her mirth a tremulous bitterness
That jarred unnatural in such an elf
Of freak and sportiveness; and most of all
When she was bitter she was tender too,
Yet hard when she was simply gay. She fled
From strangers' presence, yet, if she was forced
To front it, bore herself, first queenly, then
With a flash and glitter of quick wit and glow
Of almost joy that proved how far she was
From the sad love of solitary calm,
And how far from uncouth sly bashfulness
Of conscious silly schoolgirls. Then her face,
Which changed its meaning at a word, would change
Sometimes another way, and sudden show
On its round girlishness a worn waned look,
As of a woman growing older. So
She angered him with changes, as you're vexed
With the symphony that hurries you away
From the sweet strain you liked to one more wild

And then, ere you are sated with the new,
Takes you at unawares back to the first.
Changed music does not tire though it may chafe,
And Lota's fitfulness was never dull.

And Gervase quarrelled with her day by day,
Till Evelyn knew he loved her; though at first
Himself he hardly knew it. Evelyn watched
With a sick heart, and trembled: once she said
"Nay, Lota, tell him." Lota but said "Why?"
And then, when Evelyn spoke, "It seems to me
He loves you," kissed her fondlingly and laughed
"Dear love, if he loves either it is you."

But she was sadder after that, at times
Half querulous, and bitterer when she laughed;
And Gervase never said nor did the thing
That pleased her. And yet once, and twice, he saw,
When she had pained him sharpest, that her eyes
Were heavy with big tears and her paled lips
Were quivering piteous. And the passion rose
Into his heart "She loves me, and *shall* love."

He waited. Lota was so strange; a word
At the wrong moment, a too happy look,
Too loving, a too confident clasp of hands,
Might startle her away from him. She seemed
A timorous wild thing, liking to be stroked,

Yet shrinking from his hand lest it should hold
Too firm for flight, and, suddenly alarmed,
Butting for very fear. " I dare not stir,"
He said, "lest I should lose her." And it was
As if, in losing Lota, he should lose
All fire of loving in him, all delight
In womanly sweet charms, in ruddy lips
That seem grown ripe for kisses, white warm arms
Waiting to cling about a husband's neck,
Clear eyes meant to look large with love, the play
Of glorious blushes flashing at a look,
The subtle stir of life in every limb
And the round grace of form—all Lota had
Less than a many women Gervase knew,
Than any of her cousins, but of which
She was to him the bodied perfect all.

He waited, meant to wait. But on a day
He brought her, simply, as he would have brought
To Evelyn or Constance, a choice spray
Of pearly hot-house roses amber-touched
Towards the core, because he heard her wish
For such a rose to draw into her group:
And Lota mocked him for the pains he took
To be a squire of dames; and first the flowers
Were over yellow for her, then too pale ;
And then she tossed them into Ethel's lap,
As just the tint to suit her that night's dress.

Till Mrs Westland, vexed, cried out at her
For such a wayward thanklessness " Indeed
Gervase is far too good to have so long
Taken your snappish ways indifferently,
And still have wished to pleasure you to-day."
Then Lota tried to laugh, but suddenly
Broke into tears and hurried from the room ;
And Gervase on the moment followed, snatched
Her trembling hand, and drew her suddenly
Into the balmy quiet, where sweet flowers
And greenness and white placid statues were,
Into the balmy quiet, they alone.

" My darling !" that was all he said, and drew
Her close to him, and close, and filled her face
With hot long kisses ; while she bent and shook
Between his arms like a frail harebell tossed
By summer tempests.   But a moment more
And she broke from him. " No, Gervase ; go from me—
No, not your darling.   Nothing, nothing to you."
" My wife," he answered, but she would not speak:
" My wife," he said again, " Speak.   Not my wife?"
But she gasped " Go.   Oh out of pity go.
To-morrow I will tell you."

                        As she spoke
The aunt flapped in, rustling against the plants
With stormy silks, and panting in her wrath.

But Gervase did not wait to learn her mood,
"To-morrow Lota!" and he hastened forth,
Hating the sound of voices till her voice
Should say the sweet shamed Yes of the sweet morrow.

And he fled homeward, laden with a hope
Which seemed too restless and too great to hold,
So that he longed for night and mindless sleep,
As if it had been pain, to keep it drowsed.
And, for some lullaby and present slack
To the strong heart-beats of expectancy,
He wove and watched the dreamer's cloudy coil
Of sweet self-histories, part shaped of hopes,
And part of things that are, and more than all
Of bright impossible grave phantasies.
He made the wedding over, and his wife
Turning to him, Undine-like, "Now, love,
My true great life begins;" and he replied
"And mine too Lota," while he took the hand
That wore his ring and kissed it; and she looked—
But the look was not forthcoming, he had seen
No such grave radiant love in Lota's eyes
As would be then, and could not picture it.
He made her cantering on his favourite Ralph,
A little awkward gracefully, and pleased
To need his teaching, while he scolded her
By way of praising, riding close beside.
He made her wandering with him in his woods,

Bidding him drag down boughs beyond her reach
Where she was greedy of the bloom, and break
The hawthorn stems that were too strong, or climb
To spoil some rugged bank down in the copse
Of its sweetest primroses; she laughing proud
To be the lady of such pleasant lands;
He, acting, "So! 'tis not your only joy
To be the lady of *me;* you love me not;"
And she with merry onslaught pelting him
With flowers that cost him so much pains to get.
He made her sitting, busy by his side
With some light stitchery or book of rhymes
That would not too much keep her thoughts from
       him,
In his favourite cosy study, while he worked
With pen and papers, changing time by time
A smile or playful word lest she grew tired.
He made her mistress of his house, or child
To play with and to tease; queen whom he served,
Or love's sweet handmaid fondly tending him;
Sudden as now, or calm for happiness;
Eager or gentle; frolicsome or grave;
But made her always his, her whole thought his.
She had told it him that day, if not in words
Nor even looks, if not by meeting hand
Nor answering lips to kisses, nor coy turn
Of head, nor subtle speaking silence, not
By any note that memory could keep,

Yet she had told him.   Lota loved him, loved
As if she dared not love him, yet she loved.
And why she was afraid scarce troubled him—
He was a Lester, had the Lester lands,
And Lota Deveril, whose father died
A half-pay major, was left penniless,
And did a little drudgework for her keep,
Making the children practise and read French
And keeping count of tablecloths and spoons:
So Gervase read her that she was so proud
She'd have no husband seem to stoop to her,
And wilfully was trampling down the flower
Of love that grew towards him as its sun,
Her flower of love that would not so be crushed.
What then?   To-morrow she would talk, but he
With just "You love me, what is all the rest?"
Would put it by.   To-morrow!

                And the night
Which he had longed for came before he knew,
While he thought of to-morrow, came and went,
And the to-morrow broke on him asleep,
And startled him with sunlight.

                At the aunt's
There was a fluster and the after-breath
Of household gales still fretting in the air:
Constance had wept; and Ethel's cheeks were hot

And scornful; and, with drooping curves of pain
On her set face, with heavy patient eyes
Of one who waits a better time to weep,
Silent and pallid, Evelyn sat and sewed
As if a life hung on her every stitch:
And the aunt was all a-tremble, with some speech
Quivering upon her lips that would not come;
And every now and then she gave a cough,
Grew red, and puckered up a solemn face,
Then looked at one or other of her girls,
Then coughed again, and changed her mind, and said
The day was very warm—no, she meant cold.
Till Gervase, chafed, resolved to raise the storm
That he might sooner lull it. "For," thought he,
"She plainly thinks she caught me yesterday
Cheating her niece with lying fooleries."
He looked her in the face no whit abashed,
Asked "Where is Lota?"

　　　　　　　　There was such a hush
As comes in summer when the sky grows close
Against the trees before the first gust bursts
Of the oncoming tempest, and the click
Of Evelyn's needle sounded noisily—
Evelyn who neither paused nor drew long breath,
After a moment's pause, as the others did,
But stitched on faster.

"Lota!" gasped the aunt,
"Are you so shameless?"

    Gervase, ill content
Because he thought "What! dares she count the girl
So far below my marrying she'll scold
As if our love were wicked?" yet forbore,
Choosing to seem as if there could no slight
Be meant against his darling. He but asked
"Where is my Lota?" with a firmer stress:
Then Mrs Westland shook and stammered, half
As if she'd storm and half as if she'd cry:
"Now Gervase, tell me—it is hard to ask;
I cannot think it of my brother's child—
Has she not told you how she stands? You know
Her history?" Now he knew no history,
But thought that he knew Lota. "All," he said
Indignantly, "that I need know, I know,
And will hear no more but from Lota's self:
Now let me see her."

    Ethel at the word
Broke in with passion "Dare you flout us so?"
And Constance's swelled eyes brimmed with new
   tears;
But Evelyn spoke up quietly and strong,
"Ethel you cannot know what Gervase means;
There is some secret which we do not know;

I trust in him and Lota." Gervase cried
"You have spoken safely, Evelyn, in that:
But there's no secret, and I ask to see
My Lota."

       In this while the flurried aunt
Had sat uneasy, having more to say,
And yet not knowing what. With nervous stir
She rose "Nay Gervase, come and talk with me."
He followed; but his anger was white hot,
Ready to scorch a finger laid on it.

  Then in her pink boudoir the scared dame threw
Her throbbing plumpness on a velvet throne,
And sat to preach at him: "You say you know
My niece's history?"

         "I know your niece,"
He broke in on her, "Let me hear no more
Of histories. Let Lota tell as much
As suits her and as little as she likes.
Where is she? Call her."

         She in panic shook,
And scarcely could reply; yet made a show
Of boldness. "Lota? Lota is not here.
Has she not let you know so much by now?"

"Not here!" he answered slowly, drawing breath
With the desperate calm of passion, "Lota gone!
Where shall I find her?"

              "Nay, how should I know?
She would not be reproved, she would not give
One promise to her good, she'd be left free
To go her lawless way...or leave my house.
Was I to ask her pardon, bid her stay
And have as many lovers as she pleased,
With my girls under the same roof?"

                    He stopped
Her breathless clamour, "Tell me where she is."

"How can I? Not a hint she deigned to give.
Evelyn was weak enough to ask her; she,
So artful, was not weak enough to tell.
I fear she'll let *you* know."

                "Be still," he cried,
"With your unholy taunts, your lying taunts.
Oh shameful woman, cruel, foul in thought,
How dare you spatter mud on the pure snow
Of a girl's innocence? Your brother's child!
How dared you with your stabbing poisonous tongue
Harry her out in the world you know not where—
A helpless girl."

"Girl! girls of twenty-six
Are so far on as to know wrong from right."
So she broke in.

But Gervase cried out still
"How could you do it? Women have such heart!
Show them another woman in a fault,
It is to show your terrier dog a rat—
Harry and tear and kill...'tis their good luck!
A rare day's sport, and all in duty's way!
But you, you made the fault. What fault was there
In love like ours?" She said "There was no harm
If you had been the first, but since"—He took
No heed, seemed not to know she spoke: "Aye so
You've hounded her into the streets to beg,
Or starve for what you care. I'll never breathe
The air that you breathe, seem to know your name,
I'll never hear a word of you or yours,
Till I have my own Lota. You shall ask
Forgiveness of her yet."

And so he went
In haste and heat, while she cried after him
"Oh you are mad or cheated."

Evelyn stood
To speak a little word to promise him

That she was Lota's friend, but he dashed past
And could not see her with his angry eyes.

So friendship snapped; and Gervase turned his back
On that familiar house, and left behind
Uneasy sorrow. But the aunt made show
Of only anger—Lota was henceforth
No care of hers; let her go where she would;
She never could be one with them again:
And Gervase, wilful, wicked as it seemed,
Was such a man as must be kept aloof.

And Ethel chimed in so; and Constance sighed
And hoped and wondered and condemned by turns;
But Evelyn always said "There is no harm,"
Chafing her mother who, kind at the core
But of harsh judgment, easily accused,
And, loving justice, hated to be taxed
With a rash verdict, and would score up proofs
From every trifle said or done or dreamed
To keep herself convinced of what she urged.
And then too Gervase had given some hard words
Which rankled, and it was a present balm
To think the worst of him...a leper left
To his shunned way, apart from her and hers.

II.

AND Gervase only thought of Lota, lived
In a long search for her. At morn he thought
"Will she not let me know to-day?" at night,
"Well, it will be to-morrow:" till at last,
Like some sad watcher by a sick man's bed,
Who, having hoped too much, droops suddenly
Into a blind despair and turns averse
From any comfort, he, at one new touch
Of disappointment, instantly fell numb
And sullen in his heart. "Vain, vain, and vain!
Why do I seek her? She has found some home
Dearer to her than mine would be." And yet
He did not cease to seek her. But it was
The weary task of him who will still seek
Along a great sea-shore for one he saw
Drift out upon the tide a week ago.
"Not mine, if I should find her—no not mine!

Or else no bitterest pride could make her kill
My life and hers with silence for some taunts
Which are no guilt of mine. Yet I must seek,
Lest she should be at buffets with the world;
Too rough a game, poor darling, for your strength,
Whatever fault the woman knows of you,
Who talked of histories." And sometimes he
Would ask " Had she been fettered in her youth
By some rash troth, made at her father's will,
Obeyed now, for his sake, too faithfully?"
And ofttimes he would dream her fervid mind,
That kept a subtle breath from foreign lands
Of faith unprotestant, as garments keep
A clinging sense of the rich incense mist,
Had hurried her to some wild saintly vow
Of maiden-living or, (so rash she was
To any impulse), even of convent bonds.
But never could he picture any chance
Upon her life, nor purpose set in view,
Nor bait, nor bugbear, hurrying her flight,
Which could show baseness in her. She remained
To him the same sweet April blossom, touched
With sun and rain by turns, danced in the wind
Of a gusty springtime; but in sun or rain
Or flickering shadows of the windy days,
Glowing in light or glimmering in shade,
Still perfect to its natural pure tints,
White at the core and rosy in the blush,

15

Dull days, dull weeks, dull months dragged on, to him
Seeming all void because made void of her.
The summer came and wooed him to the hush
Of woodlands, or to the wide breezy shores
Where the waves make swaying music for the dreams
Of waking sleepers gazing out to sea,
Or to the keen strong joy of eager steps
Toiling upon the scarps of snowy peaks.
But Gervase watched the stir and moil of streets,
And the great daily eddies to and fro
Of busy brattling human lives, and thought
" Lota is somewhere in the crowd."   Then once
He, wearying slowly through his dusty walk
On the baked flagstones, saw a face glimpse out
From a dingy cab, and thought " *Could* it be she?"
And in a moment smiled to think what cheats
Fancy can put on over anxious eyes.
And yet, that nothing might be left undone,
Took hastily a fellow dingy cab,
And followed closely.

          So he shortly came
Into a railway Babel, echoing
With thuds of packages, and clattering trucks,
And runnings to and fro, and shouts, and bells,
And shrieks of sputtering engines.   In the press
The face flashed out again,—not long enough—

And still flashed out like Lota's, and he caught
The colour of a ribbon and the flow
Of a loose mantle, and so pushed his way
In the wake, with them for pilots of his chase.
And yet he could not see which seat she took
In the train that throbbed already with the start
When he sprang into it. A minute—less—
And she and he were on their whizzing way
To where he knew not, though his ticket said
A far enough long road.

                    He watched and watched
At every halt for a good hour : the cloak
And lilac ribbon never came in sight.
Then, on the left, there showed a spire or two
Above a sprinkling of grey houses stretched
In straggling streets along a gradual slope,
And the train stopped again where the white board
Said "WOODLEY." And while the uncouth blurred shout
That should have been the place's name still rang
Along the platform, he saw suddenly
That Woodley was his journey's end. He saw
Just not too late, and so the train hissed past,
Clanging and rattling on towards the north,
And left him in the quiet.

                    Now his way,
The ribbon guiding still, was through the lanes

And leisurely spruce streets, with here a step,
Here a front garden or the doctor's porch,
Of rural comfortable Woodley where
There seemed no hurry, as if every one
Had thriven long ago and, now content,
Took business cosily, as a good way
Of killing time and happening on one's friends.

Gervase kept well aloof, for he had seen
This Lota's likeness was not by herself,
But with a broad short woman, elderly,
With something of the peacock in her gait,
A homely matron in a changing silk
Bulged out with flounces, and an azure tuft
Of roses or of dahlias quivering
On the satin thing a Madame milliner
Would shriek to hear called bonnet. Gervase said
"Not Lota, no. That dame of Valentines
Proves the younger one not Lota." Yet a cry
"Oh Lota, Lota, turn and speak to me"
Rose in his heart. Then too a subtle grace
Of rippling equal movement, a swan curve
Of the slight neck, a rapid easy turn,
This way or that, to look or speak, seemed strange
With the strangeness of a once familiar thing.

Six small squat houses, each with its three feet
Of garden walk and cheesecake centre bed

Fragrant with stocks and wallflowers and sweet pinks,
Each with its bright green palings, bright green door,
And bright green trellis—this was Berkeley Place.
And at the last green gate the women stopped,
But the dame of Valentines went on again,
Rustling all over with her goodbye nods;
And the other lightly ran into the house.
So Gervase sauntered past. A small brass plate,
"Madame Guarini" on the door, a bill
Of lodgings in one parlour-window—so
Entrance seemed easy. Could it be ill-viewed
If he should ask what lodgings there might be?
Madame Guarini might perchance reveal,
Unconsciously, the answer which he sought
To a far other question.

               At a word
The little flurried maid unclosed the door
Of a small grey-green room. "In here, sir, please."
No one was there, and no one came. He learned
The patterns on the drugget and the walls,
The different tints of fading on the chairs,
The names of the few books, the oftenest note
In the twitter of the two brown bright-eyed birds,
The number of the blossoms on the plants
In the square narrow window; unawares
He learned them, then there was no more to
      learn,

And he perceived he was forgotten there,
And tried the broken bell a dozen times,
And then for patience sake took up a book,
A little foolish novel.

                    Thus it chanced
That she was in the room before he knew.
She, Lota! "Gervase! Gervase here!" she gasped
And seemed struck helpless. Then, her face aglow
With a delirious triumph, her eyes bright
With sudden tears, she sprang to give her hand.
"To think I did not *feel* that you were here!"

    But Gervase looked at her unthankfully,
"Am I so welcome? Yet you left me Lota."
Then her face changed, as, in clear sunset eves,
The snowy hill-tops change when the last flush
Wanes silently into a mournful grey:
She said "I had forgotten," and her voice
Was weary and asleep: she said but that,
"I had forgotten," and she turned from him
And threw herself into a listless ease,
Sitting apart.

            "Forgotten what" he said
"That should have been remembered? Lota, speak;
What is your secret? Why do you hide here?
Or tell me first but this, are you alone?"

"Hide, do I? Nay it was before I hid,"
She answered with an angry carelessness,
"And, for my secret, I have none left now :
And, for alone, I have my little rooms,
And pay my little rent, and earn it first—
And so far am alone. But I have friends—
If that's your question—two kind honest friends
Who helped me to my independence here,
Good friends who never taunt me."

                    Then she broke
Into her passion : "Gervase, do you think
I should have tamely waited—what! with her?
If she had been a stranger, yes, perhaps.....
Till the morrow. But my father's sister! she
To preach of dangers, shame, I know not what;
To warn me, set me up a bugaboo
Of what the world would say, to sob and rave
And taunt and sneer and rate me for light ways
As if—as if I were not who I am.
See, I am not patient yet: I do not care
To be patient at *some* wrongs."

                  "But I"—he said.

"But you," she broke in eagerly, "I know
What you will say; you never did me wrong.

Ah! no; it is for you to pardon me,
If you *can* pardon. Gervase, never think
That I forgot you loved me, did not care.
Oh! I was base towards you, keeping so
My cold disloyal silence, I was base:
No hottest cruelest long pain of pride
Stung by her dreadful blame should have prevailed
Against my yearning once to speak to you,
Once, if by no more than dull written words,
To—

"Gervase, Gervase let me say it now,
All I *may* say. Forgive me, oh forgive!"

And with that cry she slid down to the floor,
And so, half lying with her face hid close
Against the cushion of her chair, sobbed out
With quick convulsive weeping, "Let me be"
She cried "Oh let me be."

But Gervase still
Would soothe her, lifted her in his strong arms,
Smiled in her face and kissed her. "My own love"
He said "Do you love me? Tell me only that."

But she was silent.

"Well," he said, "still keep

Sweet silence, I will think it is a yes."
Then she cried weeping "Oh! I love you well,
Too well, but never talk of love again :
Be pitiful."

    He said "My foolish love,
I know you have some vexing tale to tell,
Which for your comfort you shall tell : but first
Promise me this much trust—if I shall say,
When I have heard it, that I hold you free,
By justice and by truth to yes or no
At your own will, you 'll say my asked for yes."

 She looked at him as though she heard him speak
Some unfamiliar tongue reaching her ears
Without a meaning. Then she hid her face
In her trembling hands, " You do not know it then?
They did not tell you! Gervase do you not know?"
He said, " Nay, I know nothing...only this
That I trust you, knowing nothing, and I love."

 Then she uplifted to him a wanned face,
And told him slowly out of trembling lips,
" I have been married ; and he was not dead."
And he was still as if she had struck a blow
That dazed him into stupor, and they sat
In a numb helpless silence, face to face,
And did not see each other.

Then at last
He rose and paced the small room to and fro
Like the impotent chafed lion in his cage,
Resting himself with fretful restlessness.
Till suddenly he stopped, "Tell me," he said,
And said it patiently, so that she thought,
"How great he is, he has forgiven me."
And longed the more to tell him her whole heart.

She said, "But only do not look at me
And I will tell you, tell you with the truth
Of deathbeds. I would have you to the most
Know me as I have lived, as I have borne,
And been made desolate of every hope,
Of every love-sweet womanly dear hope,
For all my life. You'll judge me tenderly?
I did not feel how we were drifting on,
You and I ignorantly drifting on,
Along a treacherous stream that presently
Would whirl its eddies round us, suck us in.
Gervase, I did not think you loved me; no,
Not till it was already half too late.
You will not think I kept you in the dark
That you might darkling love me, will not think
I lured you, I the wicked siren, proud
To whelm so strong a life into my waves,
I the fond selfish elf-thing caring not
What weary weird I brought upon your life

If mine might be a little while made rich
By you, by your love, by my loving you.
Oh Gervase, judge me tenderly; my sin
Of silence was a great one, but not that.
I did not think to wrong you, no not that."

"I know it, Lota," Gervase answered her,
" I know—I'll no more blame you than I'd blame
The cloud from which a fork of lightning shot
And struck me blind and palsied. Let my wrongs,
If wrong there be, go by, and make me know
Your own sad story only."

                              "Ah !" she sighed,
"It means no more than what the door can tell—
Madame Guarini—Did you see it there ?"
"But not as *your* name ?" he replied, "I thought
It was the woman of the house."

                              "My name,"
She said, "My name which I bear frankly now,
And know no risk, not even the risk it brings,
Is worse than an hypocrisy. When you
Knew Lota Deveril you knew a liar;
I left that name behind me nine years back,
With my free foolish girlhood. Nine years back !
It seems as if some other lived, not I,
In those far days, and was a frightened bride,

But not unwilling, hardly quite unwilling.

"We were in Venice then—my father liked
The life there, and we always lived abroad
Because he said he would be poor in peace
And have a poor man's pleasure when he liked,
And that, in England, all his neighbourhood
Would play the sentinel upon his ways,
And keep accounts for him with shaken heads
At this too spendthrift, that too miserly.
And I too loved the freedom; no strait walls
Of meaningless dull custom prisoning us
Into the limits of our neighbours' lives;
No fashion stricter on us than we chose,
No laws forced on us, to look grave or laugh,
To be alone and quiet, or to talk
And simper friendliness, to walk or rest
At due fixed times. It was an easy life.
But we had friends, and made no sullen choice
Of loneliness; I laughed and danced and sang,
Like other girls, on many a merry night,
In many a great quaint palace where the ghosts
Of its old-world lords flit by in quiet hours
And know their way, there is so little changed.
And so he met me, and he would not rest
Until he knew my father. And he tasked
His whole great skill of gracious courtesies
And flowing talk made rich with noble thoughts

And subtle reverent flatteries, to win
His easily won trust.   My father was,
As the bravest men are oftenest, a man
Most like a woman in his heart...and that
Means that he could be duped by any mask
Of honour or of kindness.   So he learned
To love Emilio blindly.

                " Very soon
We knew I had a lover.   I was scared.
The thrill was strange to feel his deep fierce eyes
Burning upon me, not to be escaped
Shrink in what nook I would.   His changeful voice,
Now passionate with praise, now low and sad
Like the murmur of the pine-woods from far off,
Pained me as sweetest music pains the ear
That longs for stillness.   Then the rush and stir
Of angers in his talk, when he cried out
On wrongs of Italy, on this man's fraud,
That other's cowardice or callous sloth,
Jarred on me like a madman's eloquence
Until I almost feared him, though they made
A hero of him to my childish mind.
I was scared and wished he had not loved me, yet
Was proud so to have pleased him, and I thought
'Nay, since he loves me, such a one as he,
It is my fate to love him.   I have lived
With a child's carelessness, and am not ripe

To love with woman's love; but doubtless he
Is the strong sun that shines, and bye and bye
The flower breaks from its sheath and is ablow
And gives its richest perfumes.' And I'd muse,
In the sweet trance of daydreams, on the joy,
The perfect earnest joy, that would be mine
Of loving. I should be, I thought, like one
Who, wandering down a leafy dim ravine,
Comes suddenly in sight of the great sea
Which he has dreamed of, but has never known,
And presently is standing on the shore,
Gazing on the unbroken boundlessness,
Gazing upon an infinite new world.

  "Then once—and even then Emilio was
But a new friend—my father sat with me
One summer evening. Ah! I feel it now!
The dim sweet greyness coming tenderly
Over the cloudless sky, the gurgling dip
Of passing oars below, the hushlike sound
Of voices breaking through the stillness when
The day gives slow goodbye and falls asleep,
The scent of roses and of orange-bloom
About our windows! We sat quietly,
Thinking our twilight thoughts; but all at once
He said 'Child you have won a noble heart.
I am thankful for it; I have given consent.'
I cried 'Oh no! Too soon! I did not know!'

And he, all troubled, took my hands in his.
' How 's this my child ? You love him, do you not ?'
' I do not know,' I said, ' I cannot know,
I am afraid.' ' Ah well,' he said, and smiled,
' I know : I am not blind. And now to-day
Your Emilio spoke, and I said Yes to him,
Most cheerfully said Yes. My little girl,
I am not young in years, and in my health
Am older than my years, and I am kept
In dread of death because of you : my heart
Will have a sore weight off it when I know
You are in as safe keeping as my own,
And one more happy for you. And I 'm proud,
Yes proud, you puss, of my fine son-in-law.
I'm as happy, I believe, as you can be.'
He kissed me, and I kissed him back again,
And loved him more than ever and was glad
Because he was so glad. But yet I said,
' Am I happy do you think ? I scarcely know,
It is all dreamlike. Did you tell him then
I was to marry him ?' He laughed. 'I said
All I could say. He's coming presently
And you shall tell him what you like. But yet
I'll own he is prepared to be made wild
With happiness—such joy I never saw.'

"And almost as he spoke Emilio came
And asked no question, but said instantly,

'My Lota, my pledged wife, soul of my life,'
And took my hand, and bade my father bless us.

"Ah me! he seemed so happy, and I felt
A joy swell up in me because I was
So much to him, and, looking in his face,
I thought I loved him, and I let him put
His ruby snake upon my finger—Look
I wear it now again, it is best so.
And after he was gone I could not tell
If I was glad or sorry to be his,
But felt that I *was* his. I did not wish
To take my promise back. I was afraid
And I was hopeful; and which most I was
I know no more to-day than I knew then.

"We married. And the shadows came at once.
He seemed to love me—one might almost say
He must have loved me, he so seemed to love—
But his love was like the heated desert wind
That scorches and that stifles, like the breath
Of lush magnolias when the air is close;
I fainted in it, longed to fly away
To the cool freshness of my former days,
To the mild restful love my father gave.
My husband felt my shrinking and would swerve
Sudden in his hot love-gusts, darkening down
Into a sullen or a stormy grief,

Or flashing into some strange jealousy;
Until I shrank the more and only longed
To be away, out of his reach; as birds
Just caught and wild must try to burst the hold
Of hot strong hands that pet them. And I beat
My helpless wings and battled, as birds will,
For freedom, with a feeble wilfulness
That makes the captor angry.

               "But he seemed
Angry because he loved me, not because
He changed against me. I might yet have learned
My new life, have been tuned to that loud love
That hurt me. But, before I could begin
To love him, I was taught to scorn.

               "There came
A dreadful woman, with bloomed artful cheeks,
And deep great glittering eyes, and a false voice
That purred and coaxed, and cruel bland slow
     smiles
Quivering with hatred—a great countess she.
I knew her name and would have been well pleased
To be among the guests who weekly flocked
To see her splendours: but Emilio said
'Let the great ladies go, who smile and kiss
And then turn round and whisper to some man
New lies about her; and we men may go—

There's a fine nature in her and she's keen
And beautiful and loves our Italy—
But my wife who is a little spotless dove
Flies with no glorious prey-birds such as she.'
But the great lady came to me and said
'Your husband hides you, Sweet.   He is afraid
Some bold man's eye should see you and observe
What a new rare rose you are for lovers.   Well,
He will not bring you to me, so I come
To you.'   And then, when I had spoken her
Some faint few words of welcome, she laughed out
A hard unnatural melodious laugh;
'We will be friends,' she said, 'some women now
Would hate you, little girl, for laying hands
On a jewel like Emilio.   I forgive...
And I have forgiven him too.'

                              "And I said,
In anger, for she mocked me openly,
'I know not, Madam, what you will forgive. ·
You being married, what is it to you
What wife my husband chose?'

                              "She laughed 'Well played!
How well you drew your head up, little queen,
And threw that "husband" at me!   Aye, you think
He's yours—indeed 'tis not a many weeks
Since you gained him, as you thought, all to yourself.

You foolish child, did you not comprehend
That marriage frees a man from faith to you?
There's nothing gained by faith; for you are his
However. Lover, he had been all yours:
Husband, why he is yours or any one's.
I have forgiven him—I told you so—
And that means he is mine as much as yours.
" *My* husband " how you flung it at me, Sweet!'

"I turned from her 'Go, I'll not answer you.
'Tis shame enough that I have changed a word
With such a woman.'

           " Still she answered sweet
And soothingly 'Nay, pretty petulance,
Why are you bitter at me? Blame yourself.
If a woman weds the man she loves, whose fault
But hers is his lost lover constancy?
He takes to husband ways... 'tis natural:
You should have thought of it in time, that's all.
Why, look at me who love him, as such babes
Fed on sweet pap and comfits cannot love...
No more, dear fools, than you can hate or sin,
Me, whom your husband loves—I am content
To lend him to you or to Melanie,
The blonde French dancer, to, as scandal tells,
La Stella, the inspired...who in her songs
Puts Italy and means your husband, child.

16—2

Be patient and be happy as I am.'

"And then she suddenly threw off her glib
And cloking blandness 'Girl, I hate you—*hate!*
I came to look at my Emilio's wife,
And hate her. Aye, I'll make him trample you
Beneath his feet. If I'm not all to him,
At least I'm more to him than you could be,
And you shall feel it, you who cheated him
With silly simpers, innocent fond dove,
Who cannot coo so sweetly but he knows
There's better music and goes after it.
Do you hear? I hate you, girl. Do you hear it well?'

"At this I gathered all my pride, and looked
Full in her face, and coldly. 'Madam, yes;
I heard. It was a matter scarcely worth
Your trouble in the telling. Will you sit
And rest before you go? I say farewell,
Since you have done your errand to me here.'
And so I left her.

"You might think I sat
Brooding upon her wicked news, and wrung
With a wife's agony of doubt and hope,
With a wife's desperate disbelief. But no—
Perhaps it means that I did never love
This husband whom yet other women loved

With the whole heart in them good or bad—I felt
Only an anger hot and cold by turns,
But always anger, never simple grief,
And never, not one moment, with a touch
Of sad forgiveness. She had said of me,
That woman, that I could not hate ; and that
Was true perhaps, for I scarce hated him:
But it was truer that I could not, nay
I cannot, smile away a wrong ; it burns
New in my heart for always. I might give,
If it seemed due, my life to save or serve
A traitor to me, but I could not play
At meek forgetting. Gervase, it is strange
You can forgive me, me who cheated you."

He turned and looked at her for the first time.
"I love you Lota." Then he spoke again
Before her answer "Nay, yet after all
It should not be but that. If I am wronged,
(And, till I have heard more, I do not own it),
And if I loved you less, yet there would be
Pity for you, and—Well I will not preach:
But, Lota, not to pardon is to be
Unlikest God of any human way
In which we might be like him."

"Yes," she said,
"You are like Evelyn, who, while she talks

So scornfully and eager against wrong,
Yet seems to think that who does wrong to her
Has earned some special due of charity.
But I am bitterer and weaker."

                        "Well,
I pass to what went next. Emilio came
Soon, but I was prepared. I said to him
No word of who had been with me, I kept
A heavy silence : but, when he cried out
'Oh Lota, will you never give me back
Some little of my love?' I answered him
'La Stella loves you, is not that enough?'

   "He gazed upon me, startled: 'What!' he cried,
'The proud brave soul that will not be afraid
Of their fools' malice, though she writhes and bleeds
Under their petty stabs, could they not leave
Her name alone with you? Who spoke of her?'

   "'Her songs, perhaps,' I said, 'but you do well
To boast her so to me—to me your wife.'

   "He thought a moment then he spoke, 'It seems
I shall do well to tell you more of her.
She is a noble creature, one I'd choose
As friend for you, if it might be: I look
To have you know her. If she loved me once,

Or loves me, 'tis with such a lofty love
As she may take to heaven with her.   Yes
It shames me, for I am not worthy it,
It does not shame her.'

     " 'Yet,' I said, 'you hid
That noble friendship from me.'

       " He looked down.
' Hear my confession, love.   I have done ill,
But not to you.   I have a foolish fault,
I am greedy of all love, of any love
That comes to me, I take it as one takes
A flower from any hand for its own sweet
And not as caring for the hand that gives,
I take it womanlike.   And, as for her,
I honour her and could not but be proud
To have her, see me with a different smile
From that she turns upon so many pleased
With her least notice.   So, forgive me, love,
I found it hard to tell her of a smile
That made me happier.   But we'll go to her
You and I, dearest, and, she has a heart
So great and tender, she will love you more
Than if her brother brought you and required
A sister's love for you.'

     " 'She has a heart

That finds a use for any kind of love,
As yours does,' I replied, 'if she will take
My love in pay for hers instead of yours.'

"'Nay Lota,' he said earnestly, 'I swear
I have not wronged her once with one fond word,
I do not say for your sake, but for hers,
I have not wronged her once with one fond word.
And now forgive me, Lota—love me more.
Love me, my own, I shall ask no more love.'

"'Not Melanie's?' I answered quietly:
He sprang as if a wasp had stung him, stamped,
Hissed through his teeth. 'Gossips and fools' he
        breathed.
'Not Melanie's?' I said again. 'Perhaps
She too has a great heart with room for me.'

"'Lota,' he cried, 'I will not bear your taunts.
I am wrong, wrong here again, but do you think
You are to twit me with my least escape
From the chill misery you make me here,
Where you'll not love me, no, where you so smile
As you may upon your priest, or else so shrink
As from a lackey's touch, look bland and smile,
And yield, as if I were some visitor,
Or droop in silence like a weary slave?
Are you to twit me as if it were a crime

To try to seem a moment my old self?
What's Melanie? Should I seek Melanie,
And Melanie's light friends and noisy routs,
If you would sit with a kind hand in mine
And look as if you loved me?'

                     "'Proved,' I said,
'Your outburst shows you have no answer here:
And I could hate you. Will you teach me love
On the pattern of this dancer? I, your wife,
You tell me you, perforce, must woo this thing
Of gauze and paint until I love you more?'

    "'I do not woo her, child,' he said, 'she has
Wooers to suit her better: she and I
Know that our ways go separate through the world.
I prize her lightly, pleasantly; she laughs,
And likes me but too well, poor butterfly;
But talk of love to *her!* I could as soon
Play lover to your kitten frisking there.'

   "I said, 'For me, I never shall care more
To whom you play the lover, you who put
Your open slight upon me, you who go
In the eyes of all the world the daily page
Of a light actress.'

              "'Lota no,' he urged,

'They lied who told you so. I can count up
How often I have seen her since she came
This year to Venice, on one hand—four times
Or five in nearly twice the weeks. But yet
I blush before your anger; I did put
A slight on you for which I hate myself.
But you, you must not hate me. Oh! my wife,
Bear with me, I have little earned your love
But I will put my whole life in your hands
And you shall rule it for me.'

     "'Nay,' I said,
'I leave that to the woman who came here
And told me she was more to you than I,
And she would teach you how to trample me;
I leave you to her, she is glorious
In wicked beauty, I am but a girl
With everyday girl's brightness, and she says
I have not mind enough to sin...like her.'

"He looked at me with a white awful face,
As if a horror took him. 'Do you mean
She came to you? Olympia?'

     "'Yes,' I said,
'The countess came to me, forgave me. I
Forgive not her, nor you.'

"'She is,' he cried,
'A fiend, a beautiful fierce deadly fiend.'
I said 'She is your love.' And then he bowed
His head into his hands, and presently
He almost sobbed and when he looked at me
I saw he had been weeping...like a child
Whose cunning has been just enough to find
The way to some pet mischief, not enough
To gloze it at the need. And yet I felt
A sadness for him when I saw him thus.

"' Lota,' he gasped 'what shall I say to you?
That woman is my demon : day by day
I grow to hate her, as the drunkard hates
The draught he cannot part from ; day by day
She drugs me with the passion of her love,
And makes me weak before her. I had thought
Our parting was for ever, when I learned
My one true lesson of full perfect love—
When I loved you and knew I never loved
Another woman. But I have not known
How to make your heart beat with mine, not found
The way to make you rich with happiness
So that some drops might overbrim and feed
My thirsty love. I have but wearied you
With my poor feverish cravings after love ;
Some fine grave instinct in you doubtless spoke
To make you shut me out into the cold,

Because I had sat down by other fires
Seeking for warmth and being charred and scorched
And was not worthy to sit in your sun—
You could not love me.   And, when once we met
By chance, she guessed it in my silent face,
Which looked, she said, as if it were a frost
For want of smiles to thaw it: and she made
The old spell of her fervour strong again,
And drew me to her.   And at first it was
Like the door thrown open of a pleasant hut,
Where light and food and a blaze upon the hearth
Make comfort to a worn out shipwrecked man,
Who looked to be, if gales had not sprung up,
Welcomed that night in his luxurious home.
But afterwards it was the cabin grown
A stifling prison while the outside snows
Bank round and keep the door.   Lota, my love,
I do not love her, I would fly from her,
I would be out of reach of her wild will,
Her ecstasies and anguish.   I am weak,
I cannot spurn a woman at my feet,
But you might make me stronger if you would:
Help me, my own one.'

                    " But I was aflame
With thrice fanned wrath, because he spattered me
With his own mud-blots, flung his sin at me,
Making it *my* sin: and I started back,

Out of the reach of his hand seeking mine,
As though her touch were on it like a slime.

"But he cried on me for forgiveness, talked
Of loving me, 'Why have I been,' he urged,
'Impatient so of exile, fretting so
To take you to my Naples, but for thought
Of flying her?'

        "Then his word 'exile' struck
A doubt and made it ring: for I had mused
Why, time by time, he said 'We must go soon,
My father soon must know you,' yet the day
Of going came no nearer. For in truth
Though I had told him that it made me glad
Still to be near my father, I had made
No pleading for delay to hinder him...
Since he too had a father. On that day
I thought I had discerned the secret bar,
The witchful knotgrass thrown across his path
By that abhorrent woman. Now, he spoke
A riddle not so answered. So I drove
My questions at him, 'Do not ask' he said,
And then I pressed the more. And so I learned
The lie put on my father, dear old man,
Who stood so proud and honest—"Nay, my girl
Is worthy of the noblest of your names
In all your Italy from north to south,

But yet I'll have your father's word on it
That she is welcome, or the matter ends.
Write to him, tell him she is very poor
In purse and friends, can neither make nor mar;
Tell him what else you like, but tell him that:
Then we go by the answer.'

                              "It seems that then
Emilio wrote and pleaded anxiously
With an ungenerous father, who, half dead
For years in body, was all dead in soul,
A man who wrote, 'Why marry her, if poor
And so obscure? she might be easier had.
But, if you think of marriage, find a dower,
And, if you can, some interest at court,
Here or elsewhere. And, if you 've looked in **vain**,
I've the right woman for you here at hand;
Not ugly either, for a wife.' I think
It was in that same letter that he said,
' But, if you play this folly out, take note
You'll have my blessing, Carlo every doit
The law will let me strip you of, and that
Is nearly all my having.' I believe
Emilio wrote and wrote to him again,
And then, still answered thus, defied him. **Then**
The old man wrote, 'Thou hast my blessing **son.**
Be happy to thy liking. May thy wife
Repay thee fitly for thine ardent love.'

And that Emilio brought, and said 'Now read,
And give me Lota.' And my father knew
The old man was infirm and seldom took
The pen in his frail fingers, so he thought,
'This, written by his own unsteady hand
Shows willingness enough,' and was content.

" My husband put the letters in my hand—
They told the story, I asked nought of him.
But he was voluble with argument
How love excused him. And he dared to think
I still might love him! But I answered him
With weariness and loathing, for I thought
Of my father who would nearly break his heart
To know what husband he had given me,
My father who wore truth so near his soul
He almost lost the sense that men could lie.
And the man who said he loved me lied to him!
Lied to his shaming and to mine, that I,
His daughter, should be shown, like some poor drudge
From the kitchen or the farmyard, half abashed
And half puffed-up to be her master's mate,
Creeping by marriage up a backstairs way
Into a scornful household.

" For I was
A secret. I was hidden like a shame.
Emilio wrote some vague submission, then

Married me. And the old man took it, duped,
That, loved or left, I was to be no wife,
And chuckled at his power.

                  "'Forgive' he said:
The man who was my husband, paled and shook,
And wept to me 'Forgive.' But do you think
A woman can be patient of such wrongs
And not polluted by them? Should she smile,
Speak softly, play the sympathetic wife,
Pick her steps among the garbage, hand in hand
With a liar and a libertine? Forgive,
From wife to husband, means so much or nought.
Answer me, Gervase, you who can be true
Against yourself or for yourself alike,
Afraid of neither, could I have forgiven?"

  "You could not" Gervase answered heavily
Out of his listening.

              Lota said "So long
He made a tempest round me that I seemed
Numbed and bewildered by my weariness,
And prayed him for mere mercy to forbear
And let me have the rest of lonely thought.
And then he let me pass. But while I lay
In a half trance of stupor on my bed
I heard him come and shade away the light

Where the sunset broke in on me, and I felt
That he stood watching me some minutes long:
And then he went.

        "At night, when I awoke
From a dense painful sleep, there was a face,
Whose smiles I *could* believe in, watching me.
My father said Emilio summoned him,
With two wild blotted lines, to care for me
While he was gone. And presently we found
A little sealed up paper near my hand
'Thou hast willed it. Dear one, I am gone to force
Thy welcome from my father. Then perhaps
Thou wilt begin to pardon. If I fail
I am a beggar and I shall not dare
Stand in thy sight again.'

        "I sent no word
Of answer. What had I to write? My hope
Was but to be forgotten from his life,
His way and mine for evermore apart.
I sent no word. And many days went by
As silent of him to me as if death
Had crept between us. Then at length the news
Was blared out of loud rumour's brassy throat,
Of his new latest shame.

        "By night and day,

17

In mad repentance, he had hurried on :
Then, entering his father's house, was met
By news that the old man had yesterday
Been struck down sudden, as it seemed, with death.
But, so the servants said, as if possessed
By frenzy, he made answer in a cry
Of 'Lota! Lota! Am I then too late?'
And the next moment, by his father's bed,
Was blurting out in one great gush of words
The story of his marriage. But, they said,
The old man, keen in mind as ever, yet
Seemed to have put off every interest
Save for the one great matter of his own,
The saving of his soul. 'Oh fool!' he said,
'And twice a fool to tell thy folly now.
Well, well, I've but a little time to live,
We'll let it be as if I had not heard.
Keep thine own counsel, thou....Thy cousin makes
A very son-like nurse. Hast seen him yet?'
And then he bade Emilio read to him,
Smooth down his pillows, give him cooling drink ;
And once he murmured 'Aye 'tis pleasanter
To have one's son beside one at the last.'
And the old dame, Emilio's foster-mother,
Who kept the sick man's room by day and night,
Declared it comforted and made her cry
To see the two seem drawn so much more near
Than ever they were yet since baby-days.

"But Emilio left the old man when he slept,
And met his cousin Carlo, and told him
What errand he had come on. And there was
A will, made ready weeks ago, not signed,
Made ready to be signed, the old man said,
In honour of the marriage, if he heard
His son had married the sweet beggar wench.
And Carlo went in late at night to see
How soft his uncle slept, and sent the nurse
Old Barbara to fill a lamp with oil.
And the old man slipt off before the dawn,
And underneath his pillow was the will—
Signed in a quavering zigzag, as if eyes
And hand were past the work, but duly signed
And duly witnessed by the wondering maids
Carlo had summoned with a stealthy haste.
And the will answered to the former threat....
His blessing to Emilio, his one son,
And to the huzzy he had wed : all else
To be for Carlo.

            "Emilio, it was said
In witness at the trial, laughed aloud,
And struck his cousin 'That for the huzzy's sake !'
And there was broil and scuffle ; and the son
Was driven from his father's house while still
The father lay there.

"Then, I guess not how,
He found wild followers—some said they were
Hired brigands from the hills—and one dark night
The old Guarini house, outside the town
In lonely quiet, suddenly was roused
With long unwonted echos; trampling feet
Loud in the corridors, then threats and shouts
And the ominous clang of weapons. It was thus
My husband came back to his forfeit home.

"The servants shrank, all scared, and not too fain
To do their new lord's battle; Carlo hid;
But a servant pointed—more than one 'twas said—
And then his cousin knew the house too well.
He was haled out; Emilio made him bring
All monies he had by him—a round sum,
'Twas said, because he had been gathering in
Rentals and debts and so forth. 'Half for me,'
Emilio said 'for present urgent needs:
The rest for my good friends:' and parted it
Among his grinning men. And then perforce
Must Carlo sign him papers and a deed
That yielded up the heritage and owned
'Twas taken by injustice and by fraud.
And trembling Carlo signed, and still cried out
'Oh generous cousin do not murder me!'

"And, when he had signed all, Emilio said
' Now thou art purged we'll call thee not a thief,
And let thee answer me in proper sort
For slight upon the lady of this house,
My wife. We'll try it now, in this same room;
Now, choose thy weapon. And these friends of mine
Will bear no malice if I come to harm
In a fair fight !'

        " They said that Carlo's eyes
Gleamed red with greed of blood, and that his aim,
Most nicely taken for his cousin's heart,
Missed only by the quivering of his frame
For eagerness. Emilio wounded him,
And, when he saw him dabbled in his blood
Lie on the ground called out for Barbara
To play the surgeon. ' My wife's name' he said
' Is safe, the smirch has been washed off in blood
Of this poor sordid Judas. Help him now :
I would not have him die !'

        "And so he went,
Triumphant, with his bandits after him.
And why he sought not shelter where they sought,
But frankly in the next day's noon began
His journey back to Venice, I know not......
Excepting it were madness.

"Soon pursued,
Brought back to Naples, thrown in prison, tried,
He named his crime a justice, shewed in proof
The paper Carlo signed. 'We take no count
Of cessions or avowals under force'
The judge rebuked him. 'Nay,' Emilio cried,
'Think you 'twere possible that any force
Could make a true man write himself a knave?
But, as for me, it little matters now
What you will judge: I am judged otherwhere;
And if you'll let me die 'twill somewhat serve
To make me pitied in an afterthought,
And will be charitable good to one
Whom I *have* wronged—to one whom I wrong now
By only living!'

"But there was no talk
Of death for him; though all his many friends
Could not undo his sentence—truly no
For Carlo had friends too. Condemned for life
To the galleys!

"Gervase, had you known so much,
You never would have loved me—not I mean
If else you might have loved me. Convict's wife
Or convict's widow, 'tis all one in shame."

He smiled at her, his smiling sad beyond

Her tears, "I might have said so long ago,
But, knowing you, I never should have said it,
But, knowing you, I cannot see the shame."

"Ah well" she said "it seems to me that now
Using his name, using my husband's name,
Wearing his very ring that owns me his,
Letting my honest friends here talk of him
Or not talk as it lists them, I endure
A penance that may punish me enough,
A penance that may punish me for you
As I would fain be punished. Oh, sometimes
I hug the shame because it is so great."

He said "Mad Lota, Evelyn once said
That you loved sorrow as the petrel loves
The storm-winds and the waves; you laughed at that,
But now I feel the meaning of the thought.
Oh! you have grief enough, why will you try
To swell its burden on you? You build up
A sorrow idol, and then lay yourself
Before its car to have it shatter you.
And in this story—let me say so much
For the man who is my fatalest bane on earth—
I see a great crime with the least of shame
That ever crime could have. Our English blood
Runs cooler in the veins, but yet, I think,
We've many a steady honest gentleman

Whose deadliest vengeance is a going to law
Would rub his hands 'Now that's the man for me,
A fine bold madcap standing for his rights
With a magnificent lawlessness.' There's yet,
With all our smugness, somewhere in most minds
A corner where the natural savage lurks:
In spite of Law and Gospel we've a thrill
For redhand justice bursting through its dams
Like a swelled reckless river from the hills
That rushes to its goal forbiddenly.
Oh Lota, if I loathe or scorn this man,
It is for his foul former wrongs to you
Which are—Child, I'll not talk of them. Go on:
You say he wished to die, yet did not die;
I should have thought—"

                  He drew a sudden breath,
Checking his words upon the very lip.
"I know," she said, "I feared so much from him.
I wrote; I urged him with my utmost stress
Of reasons and of prayers, I even begged
By pity to myself, so that he wrote
'It shall be as you will, since you'll not take
Even the service from me of my death,
Since you believe I shall be more a curse
Dead than alive. You put it mincingly
Out of a present pity for a foe
(You think me that) fallen so utterly,

But there the gist lies—even more a curse
Dead than alive, unless some seemly bout
Of sickness come to play the scavenger
And sweep me from your path. If I died so
You'd have no ghost to dog you : that would serve,
And so we'll pray for that end, you and I.'

"This is the letter see, and added here
In postscript 'Would thou couldst have said
Thy just farewell with but a little grief,
A little show of having loved me once ;
But that thou couldst not. And I thank thee much
That thou hast been the least harsh possible.'
It is the end of all he was to me,
Or I to him. I know but this much since :
He had his pardon some five years ago—
Carlo was dead then—that the journals told.

"We lived in Florence then ; but at the news
We fled to Paris, safelier out of sweep
Of chance winds blowing him upon our track,
And it was there my father died—ah me !
My dear dear father ! never the same man
After that heavy trouble, to the last
Gentle to me, but turning a cold face
Distrustful, nearly bitter, to all else,
And oftenest silent. Sometimes he would sit
Seeming to sleep, then suddenly would hiss

A vehement word of scorn, or break aloud
Into tumultuous anger. Even in sleep
He'd cry out on Emilio, storm at him
As basest of all hypocrites, or fret
And reason with him and rebuke, as though
He stood there claiming me for his again.
Ah me, my father! 'twas an evil day
When first you bade him come, a lurid cloud
Into the sunshine of our simple home.

"My father died; and then I did his wish,
And took my shelter at the Westlands, earned
Some part of what they gave and plucked up. heart
To bear their charity for what remained,
Because she was my father's sister. Then
I met you, Gervase. Is there more to tell?"

She ceased; yet stopped him in the answer, "Nay
There is this much—so that you may believe
I was not guilty of this pain of ours
For wilfulness—Oh! let me make you know.
I was half blinded. I had wept so much,
And then a sunshine came; I only saw
A sort of golden mist, saw not the verge
Of the great precipice to which I walked.
Oh Gervase, I was cheated by my heart,
That did not like to part from happiness;
And I believed, because I *would* believe,

Love was not love, and you and I might smile
Like sister and dear brother all our lives
And never find a miss of warmer smiles
Upon each other's faces.   I thought first
Your love was for sweet stately Evelyn,
And afterwards—ah then I would not think;
Till Evelyn said a word which I laughed off
And then remembered in a sadder mind:
And surely I *did* try to change you then—
I thought I did.   I meant to keep the pain
For me alone, and let you turn from me
With a free heart, forgetting.   Ah! my friend,
Forgive me, I would freely bear worse harm
Than any yet fallen on me, to know you
Scathless from my poor folly.   But, alas!
It is too late: the adder in the grass
Looks not too carefully what hand disturbs
Its bed in picking daisy-buds, but digs
Its fangs in the nearest flesh.   We both are stung:
Only I think that you, who have so much
To make life strong in you, will soon throw off
The last taint of the venom.   Oh, you'll find
Balm everywhere; your life is still a hope,
As lives no older yet than yours and mine
Are in their natural current; you can pass
Along a safer way and find new flowers.
Oh Gervase you, whom I made sad awhile,
You will be happy, I—"

Sudden she broke
Her cry of anguish, would have laughed it off
With a laugh that quivered twitching round the lips.
But Gervase brooked no laughter; both her hands
Were fast in his, his eyes burned into hers.
"Lota I cannot lose you! Is he dead?
Is there nothing in your heart that calls him dead?"

"He was not dead" she said; and all her face
Was curdled into wanness. Then she cried,
Writhing with an intolerable pain,
"My God! My God! do I long to have him dead?
Oh Gervase, hush! he was not dead. Oh! hush,
And let me go."

He put her gently back,
And stood away from her. "Be calm again.
I will not scare you: do not ask yourself
If he is dead or living; I will know.
And, Lota, when, as a strong faith in my breast
Assures me, I come back to you with news
That he is dead, you will be innocent,
Most innocent, of any brooded hope
To name a longing."

But she sat and wept,
And short sharp tremors shook her, as the leaves

Are shaken on their boughs by gusts in spring,
And so he asked her, "There is something yet
I would be told. By what chance are you here?"

She said, and in the answering gained the calm
He looked for, "I had in the world no friend
Truer to help me than a worthy soul
Who was our servant. She and her good man
Throve in the world, and keep the chief inn here.
When she left us to marry I had said
That on my birthday, as she asked, perhaps
Some once or twice a year besides, I'd write:
And that I did, and had such answers back
As made me laugh and cry, they were so quaint,
Showing such honest love so blunderingly.
And so I fled to her. Good creature! glad
She would have been to make me in her home
Like a fine lady daughter: but to-day
As we walked here, she turned to the old theme
And urged it with her honest eloquence.
Through her I got my pupils—I teach French,
Italian, 'fluent German,' and so forth
'Learned in the countries.'......and I do not starve."

He thought a little. "Will you for my prayer
Put strain upon your pride? I will not ask
That you should go to her, sit down again
Beside her hearth, but, if risk comes to you,
Or illness, while I am away, you'll write

To that too rashly judging aunt......whom yet
One day we will forgive together?"

                             "Nay,"
She laughed in anger, "would she care for me?"

    He said "We are in feud, for your sake now,
And for your sake, because I will not stoop
To exonerate you whom she should have known,
I will not seek her till—I told her when:
But yet, I know her, and her heart is good,
I'll trust her. Promise, Lota."

                        "Oh," she said,
"You pardon lightly, you. I am not so;
I take no grace from hands that struck me first.
I cannot tie a loop in a snapped thread
Of love, and work on with the knot and all.
You ask a promise past my strength. No, no,
I cannot promise."

                "Then to Evelyn;"
He said "You'll turn for help to Evelyn?
She did not wrong you. I could go content
If you would promise me to trust in her."
And then, because he urged it, Lota said
"Yes, Evelyn—I'll turn to her at need."
And Gervase leaving her was comforted,
As if he left her in an angel's care.

III.

So Gervase went to seek if anywhere
Tidings of Lota's husband might be found,
And thought "If he be living, it were well
To find him; for he might want even bread,
And if not, one might save him from himself
With a friend's hand perhaps: and thought again
"If he be living and were one so schooled
That he might make my dear one happy yet,
Well then, what better use could be of me
Than to have bought her happiness at last,
Ever so dearly?" Yet he seemed to know,
As by presentiment, the man was dead.

He went; and scarcely could he yet have seen
The shores of southern France wane into sky
Behind the waves, when Lota, suddenly
Fallen weaker than a year-old baby, lay

Drifting and drifting on to death. At first
She said to the good woman from the inn,
Who flounced and clattered round her busily
And cried about her, "Never fear for me ;
You'll see me strong again. Once I was thus—
Just after we left Venice last—you heard ;
I was not ill, only my life seemed spent,
Like a little brook in June whose waters waste
Till you can scarcely see a runnel thread.
I shall grow strong again as I did then ;
Just like the little brook that, drop by drop,
Gets back some life from every passing shower."
But when day after day went by and still
Each morning wakened her a thought more tired
Than last night saw her fall asleep, she said
"Nay this time I am dying," and she sent
A little pencilled note to Evelyn,
A word or two that ended suddenly
Because she was so tired. And her good friend
Wrote at the end, "Miss, she can never live
She is so weak, and she don't seem to try
But takes it as it may. Some one should come
That's fit to chirrup to her."

                              Evelyn came,
Her mother with her, but they had agreed
That Evelyn should be with Lota first,
Then tell her who besides was there. But yet

She did not tell her; but she left her side
To warn her mother. "Nay she is too weak,
I dare not let her guess that you are here.
Dear mother, when she saw you last such wrath
Was hot between you—and she is so weak.
Leave her to me until some stronger day."

So Evelyn stayed alone with Lota, watched
Her life that ebbed and flowed like river tides,
Changing but changing silently. For weeks
She watched and hoped and scarcely could be sure
If better came a little oftener
Than worse. But when the vivid autumn leaves
Showed crimson through the mist of afternoons
She knew that Lota stirred a little more
And asked more questions, and she saw a dawn
Of glimmering sea-shell pink in the wax cheeks,
And sunlights coming back upon her hair.
And Lota said, "My Evelyn, but for you
I should have shut my eyes and gone to sleep
Like the lost travellers in the snow. But you,
You kept me waking, warmed me: I shall live."

Then bye and bye she thirsted for the sight
Of grey hills through the air, and woods where yet
The leaves were lingering thinly, of quick brooks
Between the red-leafed brambles, slope-side waves
Of plumy ferns with fronds just tipped with brown

18

By earliest frosts, and flower-weeds in the lanes.
And in the sunniest hours of sunny days
The cousins lingered through the nearest walks
While Lota breathed in life from sun and air,
Like flowers, too long forgotten in the dark,
That come back to the daylight—till she said
" Why I am strong !"   Then, on an afternoon
Yellow with autumn sunlight striking low,
She said " My churchyard is not now too far—
I long to show it, 'tis so beautiful."
And so they rambled for an easy mile
Through field ways and along a little grove,
And came to a grey church with tower and porch
Half lost in glistening ivy, and the shade
Of a great cedar on its southern wall.
And westward a green slope curved slowly down
To a broad river's brim, where now and then
A barge came drifting by, but oftener
The great white swans from Yewter Hall at hand
Broke the smooth water slowly.   Down the slope,
And underneath the cedar, lay the graves
Among smooth turf, with here and there a flower
Of simple kind, set by some loving hand ;
And here and there a hedge-rose climbed and drooped,
With its wild careless trails, about a stone,
Pruned off no more than not to hide the name—
No gardener's playground this, but just so kept
As showed it was a cared for, sacred place.

And from the river's other bank there stretched
A green far plain of fields that came at last
To woodland rises, and above these peered
The grey and shadowy line of five long hills.

And Evelyn and Lota sat at rest
In the broad cedar's hush, and felt far off
From the world's hurry : and they talked of thoughts
They would not, sitting friendly in their room,
Have felt alone enough or near enough
To tell each other plainly : and at last
Lota poured out her heart.

                But, when she said
"I love him, love him still," she said besides
"I love him so that it would comfort me
Beyond all words, if he would love again—
Oh Evelyn, if he would love my friend,
And she would love him...as I think she could."
But Evelyn spoke resolute, though low,
"Not so, you dreamer. He and I no more
Could take love of our making for love's self
And keep life warm by it than we could think
We felt the rays hot from a tinsel sun
And sit to bask in it upon the stage.
Friends he and I, but never more than friends."

And as she spoke they heard a sound of steps,
And Gervase Lester, seeking them, was there,

"At Lota's door they told me where to come"
He answered to their wonderings; yet still
Wherefore he came to Woodley told them not:
But, walking slowly homeward with them, talked
Of his long useless search—till, step by step,
He seemed to lay the clue in Lota's hand,
Unwinding it as he had first unwound.

For he, when many tedious days were lost
In questionings and seekings to and fro,
Went back once more to the old Barbara,
Emilio's foster-mother, who one day
Had been too deaf to listen, and the next
Forgot if she had seen him, yes or no,
After his freeing, and the next declared
That Gervase meant him mischief, and would take
No pledge or promise from a heretic.
Gervase went back to her, with him her priest,
"Now will you take the father's word for me,
That I intend your foster-son no harm—
Good rather?" And the priest, blandly, "Do not fear,
I know his reason; tell him what you can."
And what she could was that Emilio,
Having a loud sweet voice, had gone to sing
To the rich English who, she heard, would pay

In gold for every note, and so she thought
He must be a Milordo with them now.

So Gervase went to London, seeking still;
And found a track, then lost, then found again:
And so, by fragments, traced what sorry way
The man he sought had gone.

                  Not much to learn;
Yet meaning such a countless tale of hopes
Coming and going always till at length
The very last had drifted out of sight,
Of efforts, and of languors and despairs,
Of rashnesses, and failures, and of want;
And bye and bye the recklessness that comes
From being too forlorn and out of heart:
Then sickness, and the hand of death stretched out
To take the useless life and hide it down
With those who neither work nor starve, but sleep,
And cumber no one.

                Confident at first,
Then wondering, then angry, and at last
Indifferent for very hopelessness,
Emilio made the round of London marts
For loud sweet voices, finding everywhere
The same repulse. I heard once of a youth
Whose mother in a craze had pampered him

Into the fond dream he was a great prince
Whose name rang loud upon the people's tongues,
And one day taken from her, sent to school,
He learned, poor lad, how much he was a prince,
In a hard fashion : and I who, something touched
For the poor·zany, yet could not but laugh
At the quaint error, thought "And yet why laugh?
We most of us are princes in such guise;
And some of us learn hardly in our school,
'I'm not the prince imperial, after all;
But nobody;' and some who stay at home
May never learn it...All the happier they."

Emilio learnt it very bitterly;
Because for him it meant the nighest thing
To starving.   Piece by piece the coins clinked out
From the thin purse that held his fortune : so
He must accept his downfall.   No prince he
Of opera or concert, with the gift
Out of the fairy tale to mint red gold
By just articulating; but, perhaps,
Some one would hire him for a singing drudge.
And so much grace he gained.   But things went ill:
One place his passion lost him, and the next
His carelessness; and once, when he had gained
The vantage ground of a small separate part
That might have helped him higher, he, elate,
Ran riot with some roysterers of his set,

And stood forth flurried with unwonted wine
To be chased off with outcry; so that place
Went too, and with it his last upward hope.

But yet his singing kept him in some sort
Till sickness came. Dying, almost from want
More than from ailing, helpless to turn himself,
Wasted and pinched from want and cold, 'twas thus
That Gervase Lester found him. Instantly
All care that might be, fitting sustenance,
Nursing, and doctoring, were spent on him;
So he revived; and when some days went by,
There was a letter written to, his wife,
Which Gervase saw by chance as it lay sealed.
"'Tis to my wife:" the sick man said, "she lives
At Woodley, and 'tis years since we have met.
She hates me, but a dying man may ask.
Oh! she *must* come. I cannot pray in peace
Till she says one kind word before I die."
Then Gervase said "Nay, you will startle her.
Give me the letter; I will go for you,
And bring her, if she will."

And now he came
And told this all to Lota.

But she sighed,
And trembled, and looked down reluctantly.

She said "I cannot; I should make new pain,
No other, for him." But he urged her more,
And Evelyn urged.

                She cried "Alas! there is
A hardness in me. I might shrink from him
Abhorrently when I would take his hand
And seem to soothe him. No, I will not go."

Then Gervase said "Once, Lota, while he sang,
He saw you, you who listened ignorant
Of him among an open-mouthed stage crowd,
And, when he learned your name, 'Miss Deveril,'
He threw his future wildly to the winds,
That then was something brightening; 'Lost' he said
And—thus he told it me when I had said
I would come for you, he told all unaware
That I had known you—like a desperate wretch
Who, meaning to front death, should furiously
Quaff. heady madness, cup by cup, to make
Dying a drunkard's frolic, he, doomed still
To live, because you bade him not take rest
In his own fashion, sought for madness then
To front life with, and headlong hurried o'er
The deep scarp of his downfall. 'Lost' he cried,
And took no further thought to save himself,
But rushed into a quagmire in his way,
And felt the slimy murderous waters ooze

Over the lip and choke him.   Mad indeed,
But mad because, for all his wrongs to you,
He loved you."

            But she answered, though some tears
In spite of her went slowly down her cheeks,
" If, as I guess your tale, your quagmire means
An utterer slough of vice than yet he knew,
Your madness wickedness, is it a claim
Because he tries to foul me with his guilt,
As formerly—my fault his infamies,
My fault that he betrayed me, my fault now
His lawless shameless outburst—is it a claim
Because he adds this outrage ?" so she grew
To passion by her speaking.

                  Gervase said
"Yet hear again.   Some singing people went
To Woodley, and they told him they saw there
A woman with his name, a woman young
And worth the claiming ; thus they jested him ;
But he found earnest in it they guessed not,
And secretly he came to Woodley, saw
The name, saw you.   It seemed to him that you,
Taking thus far your wifehood back, avowed
A softer mind towards him or a thought
That he might yet uplift himself to you :
And to that toil he instant vowed himself,

And the vow is not broken—only made
Too late. Lota, it was a cruel walk,
For one already weakened and ill fed:
He never rallied from it. For some days
He tried to work, and, as he sadly tells,
Tried the first time in life to really pray;
And then he lay down on his bed to die,
Hopeless and spent."

     Then Evelyn eagerly
Took Lota's hand and looked into her face.
And Lota answered hoarsely "I will go"
And walked on silent, holding back the sobs.

And when the London evening came, ablaze
With glittering lights, Lota Guarini stood
Beside her husband, stooping down to hear
His feeble murmur "Now I will thank God,
And die. But, Lota, will you kiss me once?"

There was a sudden catching in her breath,
But then she kissed him; and she said aloud,
As if she spoke to others more than him,
"You are my husband, I will stay with you
And be your nurse, with this good woman's help."

And Gervase did not speak; and Evelyn said
"Right, Lota; yet"—and stopped; but the nurse cried

"Dear lady, no, this is no place for you—
Such people round us! such a wretched room!"
But Lota said, "Nay nay here is my place
Since there's no moving him" and with a fling
Of wonted wilfulness threw off her cloak.
And Gervase said "I watched last night—to-night
I'll watch again;" and Evelyn would not go
Although they urged her.

         So through a long night
Together they kept watch. And oftenest
The sick man slept, and, if they lost the sound
Of his thick breathing, they would stoop to hark,
And whisper "Has he passed?" And every time
He wakened they would think it was for death;
And every time he settled back to sleep
Would think "Now he'll not waken any more."
But yet the glimmering morning came and peered
Upon him sleeping, Lota's hand in his;
And the full flash of day shewed them his face
Less deathly; and it seemed as if the light
Of life had sucked new oil, might flicker on
A day or two.

        The day or two crept by,
And still Emilio lived. And in a while
They moved him to a freer wholesomer air
And fresher pleasant rooms. "Some weeks to live,

With care and cheering him" the doctors said.
And Evelyn went home; and Gervase came
But rarely. Lota watched her husband's life
Alone, and talked with him of death and God,
As Evelyn would have talked; and all the while
Her heart grew nearer both to God and him.

And the first day that she could leave his side
An hour or two, she hurried to her aunt,
And kissed her, weeping "Love me as before,
For I do love you. You have been more kind
Than ever you were wrongful." Cordially
The softened matron kissed her back; she said
"That foolish Gervase came a while ago
And thanked me that I had gone down to you
When you were dying. Did you both believe,
Because I took my eyes for guide and blamed
What looked amiss, that I could let you die,
My niece, and never stir a hand to help?
And now I did not come because I thought
You would not have me; but I'll be with you
As often as I can."

But Lota said,
"Dear aunt, I help my husband best alone."
And even Evelyn she told, "You were
My stay: but I have learned from you, and now
I am his stay. Dear, we are best alone."

So she did wifely duty to her best,
And comforted and tended. And one day
When Gervase came for news, she went to him
With a pale radiant face, where a grave joy
And something sorrow-like played tremulous.
She said, "There is no doubt now. He will live,
The doctors are assured, live and be well."

He said, "Days since they told me so, but thought
You should not be sure then, for fear of change.
God bless you Lota."

                    Then she looked at him
Half frightened but with purpose, spoke to him
"Gervase, O dear brave friend, friend whom I love
With love beyond a sister's but yet like,
My husband is more noble than I knew,
And, oh! he loves me, and—and I"—she looked
Away from him and spoke in a low voice,
"And I am learning a wife's love."

                              He took
Her hand that clasped his freely, lifted it
To his cold trembling lips, "We both of us
Ought to thank God for that." And then he went.

And presently his country squires were scared

With more new systems, more new enterprize,
New works upon his lands, new drains, new dams,
New cottages, new cricket-grounds, new schools,
New churches, new steam-ploughs—he ceaselessly,
Ubiquitously, busy. "Egad" they cried,
"The devil's in the man! Here he comes back
With added cent for cent of hobby power
When we all looked his town life naturally
Would take the zeal out of him."

        But before
He went from London he had made his care
To find for Lota's husband a career
And livelihood. And so, Guarini, well,
Became a city prince's clerk.

        Now pass
Some years with me, and let me show you where
There is a smooth flat sward of lake-side shore
With a great fir-coned hill sloped steep above,
And on the water rosy snow-peaks shown,
And, over mountains fronting darkly near
With blue dim shadows in their dells and clefts
And creeping up them from the lake, a verge
Of rosy snow-peaks, and just opposite,
In the shelter of one grassy slope that mounts
In soft long curves and then breaks suddenly
In a notched line of rugged table-flat

With a great pinewood precipice above,
A little Alpine village glimmers out
From the grey evening shadows.

                    One who watched
The sunset on the far-off snowy hills
Said softly "And beyond is Italy."
And Lota answered "Italy, where once
We were not happy. We will go one day,
We and our Eva, and be happy there,
In one of these dear summer holidays."
And the child Eva, busy by their side
Making Papa a harebell crown, cried out
"To Italy, Papa's dear Italy!"
And ran to tell the others, Evelyn
And Ethel and tall Hugh and Marion,
Lota's young cousin-pupils of old days.
But Evelyn did not hear her: Evelyn sat
Apart beneath a nut-tree, and by her
Was Gervase speaking very earnestly
And low; and Evelyn smiled.

                   "Ah! once," he said,
"The day I found you in the churchyard where
I sought your cousin Lota, I heard words
Which did not name me, and yet I believed,
I scarce know why, they were of me. You said
'Friends, he and I, but never more than friends.'"

She said, and her soft voice was happy sweet,
"You did not love me then." And then she rose
And stole away alone.

                And Gervase, wild
With sudden boisterousness, caught the child up
And tossed her in his arms and carried her,
She shrieking with her mirth. " Kiss me," he said,
"A kiss for Cousin Gervase. Eva, come
Let's race each other in before the rest.
We've news to tell the Aunt—such happy news!"

By the same Author.

DRAMATIC STUDIES.

BY

AUGUSTA WEBSTER.

Opinions of the Press.

" They are studies of character, passion, feeling, rather than
of incident; yet they describe mental and imaginative phenomena
with a power and clearness which are often wanting in descrip-
tions of plain matter-of-fact......... The most striking study is
perhaps that which is called 'The Snow Waste,' and describes
in allegory the penalty of the heart which, having shut love out,
is itself shut out from love and lies in darkness. Poets and
painters have both represented cold as an instrument of penal
torture. Do our readers remember Gustave Doré's ice field,
over which Dante and Virgil walk together among the heads of
the wretches frozen into it? Even there, according to both poet
and illustrator, human passions can glow with terrible fervour.
But Mrs Webster is more consistent; her penal snow waste

excludes the heat even of immoral emotions: the wretched sufferer tells the tale of his crime with a 'dull, dreamy loathing,' a 'quiet nothingness of gaze,' in 'shadeless rhythm' and monotonously recurring rhyme. The cold has eaten into his soul. The whole poem leaves behind it an impression like that which Edgar Poe might have produced if he had been as free from erratic impulses and as inflexibly moral as Wordsworth."

—GUARDIAN.

"It must be a very subtle imagination that can conceive so extremely terrible, and yet so chaste and complete a story as we have in this 'Snow Waste.'"—SUNDAY GAZETTE.

"They are powerful, original, and full of deep and some-times passionate earnestness....The earlier poems, 'A Preacher' and 'A Painter.' are very remarkable for the care of the mental analysis which the author has undertaken; and in both, and the latter especially, the cry which is uttered comes from the heart, and the satire upon the age is full of truth and power. Very remarkable are the 'Jeanne d'Arc' and the 'Sister Annunciata.'... Our favourite, however, is the 'Snow Waste,' a noble and imagi-native poem of which any living poet might be proud."

—READER.

"Mrs Webster's dramatic and poetic poems are of no common order. Her special line is the subjective analysis of thought and feeling.

* * * * * * * *

" 'The Snow Waste' is a grand Dantesque allegory, in which one who has been guilty, during life, of unnatural cruelty of hate,

is condemned to wander for ever in a waste of snow between
the corpses of his two victims. The effect of this 'doom of cold'
is strikingly expressed by the tale, told by the condemned, being
given in eight-line stanzas of one rhyme only—'shadeless rhythm,'
as it is called in the poem : or as elsewhere—

' ....An uncadenced chant on one slow chord,
   Dull undulating surely to and fro.' "

—CONTEMPORARY REVIEW.

" Mrs Webster's 'Dramatic Studies' are a set of soliloquies,
exhibiting a very remarkable power of mental analysis. In the
first, entitled 'A Preacher,' the supposed speaker—a highly
respected and eminently pious clergyman—complains to himself
that, though he can move his congregation to ardours of enthu-
siastic devotion, he is conscious in his own mind of a besetting
coldness, a mechanical tendency to say things because he knows
he is expected to say them, and an ever-recurring scepticism on
several important points. All this is subtly delineated, and the
distinction between conscious hypocrisy (which has no part in
the speaker's character) and the deadening effect of routine, from
which he is suffering, is very admirably drawn. In 'Sister
Annunciata,' 'With the Dead,' and some of the other poems,
the authoress shows a strong dramatic sense of character, and a
quick insight into the entanglement of motives and passions."

—LONDON REVIEW.

" A more genial companion for a July day in a shady copse
(on the *suave mari magno* principle) has not appeared this
season."—SPECTATOR.

"These, we say it with confidence, display true poetic power......Mrs Webster's 'Sister Annunciata' and 'With the Dead' exhibit, in a high degree, that power of going out of oneself and thinking the thoughts of others, which is, of course, the essential function of the dramatist. There is an amount of force, too, as well as tenderness and beauty, about some of these self-portraitures, which raises them decidedly above that common level of verse composition which is attained by so many; who, while writing for their own satisfaction, appear to think they are writing for the world.

* * * * * * * *

" 'With the Dead' is, perhaps, the poem which most impresses the reader with the imaginative vigour and dramatic force displayed. The delineation is done with a firm, unsparing, and yet delicate hand. Those entitled, respectively, 'A Preacher,' and 'A Painter,' are in another way scarcely inferior......We have said enough, we trust, to attract such of our readers as are lovers of true poetry—even though not bearing a maestro's name—to a volume as strongly marked by perfect taste as by poetic power."—NONCONFORMIST.

"As a study of the workings of a nature at once loving and lofty and skilled in self-analysis, it ['Sister Annunciata'] is very lovely and very striking. It is long since we have read anything which has moved us more. And it abounds, too, in sudden turns and changes of feeling which we should think as true to nature as they are beautiful in execution ;—little touches also and gushes of human feeling breaking in, with the exquisite felicity of a true woman-poet, across the play and counterplay of old feelings and present aspirations."—LITERARY CHURCHMAN.

"Her 'Preacher,' who thinks more deeply than he chooses his flock to know, and feeds them, half by habit, upon conventions rather than upon convictions,—her 'Painter,' who has to sacrifice his ideal of Art to the needs of the hour, and who, when he has done something better to satisfy his ambition, can only say,

'I think the world would praise it were I known,'—

her 'Sister Annunciata,' in whom is embodied the whole struggle of a young heart quickened with human love, and condemned to seek heaven not through the purification but through the stifling of its instincts,—the sad pathetic reverie of the plain girl yearning for love—'By the Looking-glass,'—are all expositions of separate individualities profoundly studied and minutely realized. Amongst these, 'Sister Annunciata' holds the foremost place. The long vigil of the devoted sister, in which she struggles to wean herself from memories of the love that *will* recur,—the touching self-sophistry through which that love asserts its life, even in the attempt to write its epitaph, and the way in which the sweet nature of the sufferer stumbles over the ruin of its hopes to a higher life, and, with a right impulse but exhausted power, falls worn-out at last on the threshold of heaven, are worthy, in point of conception, of high praise."—ATHENÆUM.

"In the several poems there is great diversity; and a singular contrast is presented by the homely good sense and shrewdness of the 'Preacher,' and by the strange morbid strength of a *tour de force* called the 'Snow Waste.'...'Sister Annunciata' is the most elaborate and finest poem in the collection, and comprises a masterly analysis of the leading motives of conventual life....The 'Painter' shows a deep, and, what is more, a delicate sympathy with a class of men often having a more thorough professional earnestness than the world will encourage or allow them to live by. 'Too Late' is a slighter and 'By the Looking-glass', a less pleasant poem; but they are both interesting from the same subtle analysis of motives and sentiments which we have already noted in Mrs Webster."—PALL MALL GAZETTE.

"Mrs Webster shows not only originality, but what is nearly as rare, trained intellect and self-command. She possesses, too, what is the first requisite of a poet—earnestness. This quality is stamped upon all that she writes. The opening lines to the poem of 'A Painter' prove that she thoroughly realizes what Art means, and at once give an earnest of the power which the conclusion fulfils."—WESTMINSTER REVIEW.

London and Cambridge:
MACMILLAN AND CO.

Also by the same Author.

THE PROMETHEUS BOUND
OF AESCHYLUS.

LITERALLY TRANSLATED INTO ENGLISH VERSE.

BY

AUGUSTA WEBSTER.

EDITED BY

THOMAS WEBSTER, M.A.
LATE FELLOW OF TRINITY COLLEGE, CAMBRIDGE.

Opinions of the Press.

"Amongst recent translations of poetry Mrs Webster's 'Prometheus of Æschylus' claims a high rank. Of her volume of original poems we have already spoken. Her translation is marked by the same high qualities, but especially by fidelity to the original without losing its spirit.......We sincerely hope that her translation will introduce many English readers to one of the greatest dramas ever written."—WESTMINSTER REVIEW.

"For a lady to translate Æschylus is no longer a strange phenomenon. Mrs Browning made two versions of this very play, the Prometheus; one for her private friends, one for the

8

public. Miss Swanwick has published within the last few months an entire translation of the Orestean Trilogy. Mrs Webster had, perhaps, the advantage of both her lady predecessors, as well as of most of the translators of the other sex, in closeness and simplicity, combined with literary skill."

—ATHENÆUM.

"It has clearly been a labour of love and has been done faithfully and conscientiously."—CONTEMPORARY REVIEW.

"We have been often quite amazed at the extent to which she has complied with the severe conditions imposed on herself."—NONCONFORMIST.

"The translation may be regarded in its entirety as a really marvellous performance; it is astonishing how a certain poetic majesty for which the original is remarkable discloses itself in the choral portions and the monologues....The scholar will acknowledge the difficulty of the task undertaken, and will be struck with no infrequent surprise and admiration at the art and ingenuity with which troublesome passages are handled."

—ILLUSTRATED LONDON NEWS.

London and Cambridge:
MACMILLAN AND CO.

CPSIA information can be obtained
at www.ICGtesting.com
Printed in the USA
LVHW081341251019
635351LV00005B/8/P

9 781358 845369